# how to succeed as an
# INDEPENDENT
# CONSULTANT

# OTHER TITLES FROM KOGAN PAGE

*Consultant – Market Yourself: Raise your profile and attract new business*, Robert Gentle (2002)

*How to be Your Own Management Consultant: Consultancy tools and techniques to improve your business*, revised edition, edited by Calvert Markham (2001)

*The Guide to International Management Consultancy*, consultant editors Barry Curnow and Jonathan Reuvid (2001)

*Management Consultancy: A handbook for best practice*, second edition, edited by Philip Sadler (2001)

*The Top Consultant: Developing your skills for greater effectiveness*, revised third edition, Calvert Markham (2001)

# how to succeed as an
# INDEPENDENT
# CONSULTANT

*work with your clients & promote your business*

## TIMOTHY R V FOSTER

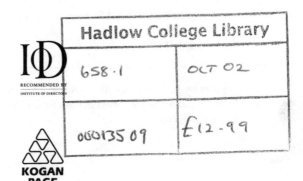

IOD
RECOMMENDED BY
INSTITUTE OF DIRECTORS

KOGAN
PAGE

First published in 2002

Parts of this book have been previously published as *101 Ways to Succeed as an Independent Consultant* and *101 Ways to Get More Business*.

Kogan Page Limited
120 Pentonville Road
London N1 9JN
www.kogan-page.co.uk

© Timothy R V Foster, 2002

**British Library Cataloguing in Publication Data**

A CIP record for this book is available from the British Library.

ISBN 0 7494 3866 5

Typeset by Jean Cussons Typesetting, Diss, Norfolk
Printed and bound in Great Britain by Biddles Ltd, Guildford and King's Lynn
*www.biddles.co.uk*

# Contents

To Stephanie

# Introduction

This book is based on my 40-plus years of experience working for companies and as an independent consultant in the areas of advertising, marketing, sales, public relations and training, in the UK, Canada and the United States.

It is designed to convey some of the ideas and techniques that I've found to be effective in developing and building business for myself and my clients. The book does not cover business structure, finance, taxes, human-resource issues or legal matters.

What is a consultant? One type I've heard about is based on the following interchange:

---

*Client:* What time is it?
*Consultant:* May I borrow your watch a moment? Now what time would you like it to be?

---

I hope you can do better than that! (I understand in Florida now there are leisure consultants – people who give advice on how to spend your spare time now you've retired to the sunshine state!)

You might be a management consultant, an architect, a writer, a trainer, an engineer, a product-placement expert, a designer, a stylist, a musician, a 'dress-for-success' specialist, a financial adviser, a computer-systems analyst or something else – if your livelihood is based on your ability to seek, obtain and serve clients, you'll find strategies and techniques in this book to help you be more successful.

# HOW TO GET THE MOST OUT OF THIS BOOK

It's organized into 15 chapters:

1.  How to create your own success plan.
2.  How to build your own credibility.
3.  How to come across as a success.
4.  How to distinguish yourself.
5.  How to know your customer.
6.  How to promote what you do.
7.  How to keep in touch.
8.  How to demonstrate commitment.
9.  How to build your credibility even more.
10. How to grow the relationship.
11. How to handle different relationships.
12. How to work with your clients in the development stage.
13. How to work with your clients in the ongoing stage.
14. How to work with your clients when you have problems.
15. How to make money.

The ideas outlined here are real, based on real experiences. All the anecdotes really happened. The mechanisms described here are not intended to be rigid rules. They are meant to be idea prompters;

allow yourself to apply variations as you see fit. Start by reading the book through, from front to back. That shouldn't take you more than a couple of hours. Have a pencil or highlighter to hand. When you come across a technique that seems to be useful, circle it. Dog-ear the page. Then go back and see if you can adapt those ideas to your way of doing business. Use them as a launching pad. Some of the ideas may appear familiar to you. Fine. They are there for completeness, so you don't miss anything. But I guarantee that some of the concepts will be new to you, and I hope you find these helpful in bringing you the success you so richly deserve.

# 1

# How to create your own success plan

Planning is one of the most important tasks you can perform in your role as an independent consultant. The alternative is reacting. With planning you can control the outcome. With reacting, the outcome controls you.

I used to be a flying instructor, but instead of teaching people to fly I specialized in teaching people who were already pilots to fly twin-engine aircraft and to fly by reference to instruments rather than by looking out the window. Instrument flying in a light twin, such as a Beech Baron or a Cessna 310, without a co-pilot, calls for intense concentration and situational awareness. You cannot allow distractions. You are travelling sometimes as fast as 220 mph and sometimes as slow as 120 at different points in the flight and you can't pull over to the kerb and figure things out. You are moving forward, like it or not, and you are operating in three dimensions, because your altitude is also critical. You are not only required to keep the aeroplane right side up; you have to navigate from point A to point B accurately, to very tight tolerances.

There is only one way to do this type of flying. *You have to stay ahead of the aircraft.* Every action you take – reduce power, start descending, retune a radio to the next frequency, extend the flaps 10 degrees, lower the landing gear, talk to the air traffic controller, turn to 146 degrees, close the cowl flaps, brief the passengers for landing, and so on and so on – every step, must be preplanned so that when the right moment comes you do what you're supposed to do without wondering. You must plan to recognize a series of moments as triggering events calling for action. 'When I cross the outer marker, I need to be stabilized at 140 mph. I will lower the gear and hit the timer. I will be in descent, crossing at a minimum of 2,500 feet. I will be on course and on the glide path and will fly the aeroplane so as to stay there.' You stay ahead of the aeroplane by planning. It is literally a life-or-death process.

It's no different for independent consultants: perhaps not quite so life-threatening if you get it wrong – but planning ahead is still very important.

Use the concepts in this chapter to create your own success plan. Here you'll find a suggested format, section headings and a case history of an actual plan that is in use today.

I had the good fortune to work at Procter & Gamble for six years in the early part of my career. P&G is famous for its 'memo'. An article in *Dun's Review*, listing P&G as one of the five best-managed companies, made the following statement:

> The manager who intends to get a piece of the lucrative P&G pie first has to learn to write the P&G memo, a brief report considered essential to analytical thinking. The idea, of course, is that if a manager can put his or her thoughts down on paper in a concise and orderly fashion, they are, in fact, rational and orderly thoughts. Conversely, if the recommendation or analysis contains illogical elements, they are immediately apparent. Memos by the typical trainee, who writes reports and recommendations right from the start, are scrutinized with the same kind of care that a writer's story is blue-pencilled by an editor. One P&G executive admits ruefully, 'I had to rewrite my first memo fourteen times!'

The act of writing a lucid description of a task will, in itself, help clarify the points that need to be made and can often bring a fresh understanding of the problem. The discipline of laying out the key aspects in a logical order will help to identify gaps. If you follow the steps outlined here, you will end up with a comprehensive plan including specific action steps to be taken.

## SIMPLICITY

Even if you are writing it just for yourself or your team, avoid jargon, and don't assume a lot of prior knowledge. If you must use jargon, explain it. The first time you use an acronym, explain it. Never assume, or you will make an *ass* out of *u* and *me*.

## AUDIENCES FOR YOUR SUCCESS PLAN

Before you start, you must have an absolutely clear idea of who the readers of your document will be. Always write with the most uninformed member of your audience in mind.

In this case, let us define the audiences as:

- you;
- your mentors and advisers;
- other key players in your organization;
- business allies, backers;
- other interested parties.

## FORMAT

Here's a basic format to follow when creating your success plan. You don't have to be rigid about it. Feel free to modify as you see fit:

- title of document/author/date;
- purpose of document – an overview of the problem and the solution proposed or needed in no more than one or two paragraphs;

- situation – the core facts of where you are right now;

- background – relevant information supporting the situation;

- considerations – aspects that must be considered in evolving a solution;

- audiences – people who are impacted by the result or at whom the result is aimed;

- objective – what it is you're intending to achieve;

- strategy – by what means you intend to achieve it;

- tactics – examples of solutions and actions.

In reviewing this subject, I'm using my own business as a case study and a key source of real-life examples. It's called ADSlogans Unlimited. I created it from scratch. It is structured around a database I have built up over the past 10 years, a database of advertising slogans. You may find it helpful to use it as a model for developing your own success plan. So here's mine.

---

# SAMPLE PLAN

## Title of document/author/date

ADSlogans Unlimited Success Plan
By Timothy R V Foster, principal
Date

## Purpose of document

As a relatively new business we need to evolve a programme of strategies and activities designed to assure success over the forthcoming years. This document is an important part of the planning process.

- *Success* is defined as the creation of a viable business with sufficient critical mass to assure satisfactory revenues, a profitable enterprise that will appeal to an appropriate buyer within 10 years.

- *Satisfactory revenues* means the ability to produce an income at least equivalent to the earnings expectations of a person employed in an equivalent area of enterprise.

- *Viable business* means one that is able to survive and grow based on its own resources and activities.

- *Critical mass* means a customer base large enough to ensure an ongoing, continuous flow of business without the need for special promotions. We want the phone to keep ringing, the e-mails to keep coming in.

This document looks at all the key factors of this business and proposes relevant and effective solutions and actions.

## Situation

The advertising industry is essential to our way of life. Advertising is carried out by most businesses, either directly or through the use of advertising agencies. A key aspect of advertising is the slogan (strapline, tagline or claim), for example 'BMW – the ultimate driving machine' or 'British Airways – the world's favourite airline'.

There has never been a computerized English-language register of slogans until now. There have been several books listing slogans, mostly US ones, but they are out of date before they come off the press.

Our database has about 100,000 lines, is updated daily and is the foundation of a variety of services we offer ad agencies and advertisers based on ad slogans. There is no other English-language service like ours in the world.

## Background

Ad agencies like to see competitive ads when they are formulating advertising for clients. There are several services that offer copies of ads or commercials on an as-required basis. But none of these has a way to search taglines as we do. Until we developed our programme, the typical ad-agency solution has been to ask people within the organization if they can remember whether a specific line has been used – a real hit-or-miss approach that does not always work.

## Evolution of an advertising slogan

The key factor that drives the need for a new slogan is the intent to produce *new advertising*. New advertising is most often developed when:

- a brand's advertising undergoes *change* at its *current* agency;
- a brand's advertising undergoes *new thinking* at a *new agency*;
- a *new or revised* brand, product or service is *introduced*.

Most advertising agencies have a comprehensive *account planning process*, which typically involves answering the following questions:

- What is being advertised?
- To whom are you advertising?
- What do you know about your audience?
- What do you want them to do?
- What can you say that will get them to do that?
- How will you know it worked?
- What ideas might work?
- What is your tone of voice?
- What is your key message?

These factors produce the following needs in the development of a slogan:

- Research the brand category.
- Understand the brand owners.
- Check out the competition.
- Develop the message.
- Complete the message.
- Evaluate the message.
- Overcome possible regulatory denial of approval.

These needs are expressed below as questions from the prospect and are followed by our solution:

- *Research the brand category.*
  'What's the big picture? Who are the key players? What do they say?' Our **BizCheck** service deals with this.

- *Understand the brand owners.*
  'What makes the key players tick? Where do they stand?' Use our **Database of Mission Statements**.

- *Check out the competition.*
  'How does the brand's message compare with that of the competition?' We modify BizCheck into **PosCheck** (Pos = Positioning).

- *Develop the message.*
  'We're brainstorming ideas for a new line. What help is out there?' Our **TermCheck** service does the trick.

- *Complete the message.*
  'How can we find out if our new line is already in use?' **LineCheck** has the answer.

- *Evaluate the message.*
  'How can we measure the line's effectiveness?' Use our **Sloganalysis®** diagnostic tool.

- *Overcome regulatory denial of approval.*
  'How can we attempt to get regulatory approval for a line when it has been denied?' **TermCheck** helps here, too.

## Considerations

Advertising slogans may be identified in three categories:

- registered trademarks®;

- non-registered trademarks™;

- lines for which no trademark claim is made.

A service mark[SM] is the same as a trademark, but applies to a service rather than a product (principally US usage). Note: slogans cannot be copyrighted©.

The issues regarding the competitive use of the same or similar advertising slogans are twofold, both threatening to cost money due to damages and/or the need to discard unusable advertising:

- The danger of a claim of infringement of another party's intellectual property. This is most likely to evolve as the result of the improper use of a registered trademark, which is relatively easy to check through trademark register searches.

- The embarrassment caused by using an unregistered line that is already being used by a competitor. Harder to check... until now.

# Audiences

Audiences are:

- customers and prospects;
- media;
- influencers;
- students.

## Customers and prospects

These are people responsible for the development of advertising:

- at ad agencies, eg J Walter Thompson, Leo Burnett;
- at multi-brand organizations that advertise, eg Unilever, Procter & Gamble, General Motors;
- located principally in the United States, the United Kingdom and other parts of the English-speaking world;
- in global organizations based anywhere that use English as their main operating language, eg ABB, Philips, Siemens.

## Media

- Business publications, eg *Financial Times*, *The Wall Street Journal*, *Business Week*.

- Trade publications, eg *Campaign*, *Advertising Age*, *Adweek*, *Marketing Week*.

- Business broadcast media, eg CNBC, CNN, BBC *Working Lunch*, *Sky Media Month*.

## *Influencers*

- Trade Associations, eg IPA (Institute of Practitioners in Advertising), AA (Advertising Association), AAAA (American Association of Advertising Agencies), CIM (Chartered Institute of Marketing).

- Advertising portals on the Web, eg AdForum, About Advertising, University of Texas Advertising World, AdFaqs, Ad-Rag.

## *Students*

Business schools, CAM (Communications and Marketing Education Foundation).

# Objective

To achieve success, defined as the creation of a viable business with sufficient critical mass to assure satisfactory revenues, a profitable enterprise that will appeal to an appropriate buyer within 10 years.

# Strategy

- Plan actions based on best practice in achieving success.

- Ensure all target audiences are served.

- Be timely and up to date.

- Build an aura of knowledge and expertise in the area.

- Keep innovating.

# Tactics

- Operate an interactive, informative and effective Web site.

- Develop a communications programme designed to drive people to the Web site.

- Whenever possible, use the Web site as the reference point during conversations with audiences.

- Maintain a customer-contact programme.

So that's my success plan. I find the process of creating it very helpful in developing a course of action. I review it at least once a month and update it at least once a year.

# BORROW FROM THE EXPERTS

For further help in developing your own success plan, you could employ the process used by many advertising agencies to develop a campaign, mentioned in the above programme. I've modified it slightly to fit your role as an independent consultant:

- What services are being promoted?
- To whom are you addressing your promotion?
- What do you know about your audience?
- What do you want them to do?
- What can you say that will get them to do that?
- How will you know it worked?
- What ideas might work?
- What is your tone of voice?
- What is your key message?

To misquote Nobel Prize-winner Albert Szent-Gyorgi: 'True creativity and innovation consist of seeing what everyone else has seen, thinking what no one else has thought and doing what no one else has dared.'

# 2

# How to build your own credibility

Why do you need credibility? So you will be used. So your services or goods will be in demand. But:

- There's a lot of noise out there – 600 messages a day!

- It's a very competitive world.

- There are many hungry competitors.

- Competition comes in many forms:
  - price;
  - service;
  - quality;
  - speed of delivery;
  - uniqueness;
  - experience;
  - knowledge;
  - contacts;
  - resources;
  - brand equity;
  - what else?

Why should anyone use *you*?

# IDENTIFY YOUR UNIQUE SELLING PROPOSITION (USP)

Unless you have a USP, you cannot charge premium rates. You need to differentiate yourself, so that when people think of you they automatically build in the link to your own USP. Or when they think of your area of specialization, they think of you. Why should someone use you rather than another person? The reason is your edge. Is it because you are there? Because you have the lowest prices? Because you know more about the subject than anyone else? Because you're fun to be with? Because you're famous?

To help you with this task, try the following exercise. Write down the names of the 10 brands you most admire – cars, TVs, restaurants, services, airlines, hotels, chocolates, cosmetics, whatever. Then write down the attribute you think that each brand has that makes it so. I'll give you a few of my own favourites:

- CNN (Cable News Network) – 24-hour global television news;
- Federal Express – guaranteed delivery on time;
- Macintosh computers – intuitive, user-friendly, graphic operation;
- Virgin Atlantic Airlines – the best business-class service.

If you know who your competitors are, try the same thing for them. Then write down 10 attributes for yourself that could be used to differentiate you from everyone else. You are a brand!

When you're clear on your USP, build it into your image. Use it in your communications, your business card, your logo, your letterhead. Live your USP! It should become part of your own positioning.

# BE A SPECIALIST

If you are a specialist in whatever you do, you can offer a value-added benefit and price your products and services accordingly. If you are generic, you can only compete on price and delivery. Your credibility will be much better if you have some uniqueness that differentiates you from your competitors.

We are surrounded by niche marketing. Companies are getting leaner all the time. They are 'outsourcing' more and more. This means that organizations that can be perceived as capable of replacing the now non-existent unit, department or division can find a ready market for their services.

One computer company near London did away with its shipping department and invited Federal Express to come in and run it as one of their branches. Many large organizations contract out their catering. Offices have people who come in and water their plants on a regular basis. Many companies have their car fleets managed by an outside agency. Some big firms have a brand-name travel agency occupying space on the 28th floor to serve all their travel needs.

All of these outsourcees are specialists. They do one thing or series of things, they are expert at what they do and they have an understandable pricing structure.

What does this say to you? Are you a specialist? Do you call yourself a specialist? Could you? What you do and how you describe it has a lot to do with your positioning.

## UNDERSTAND YOURSELF: WHAT DO YOU DO?

You're in the window seat – 4A – in business class on your way to a client meeting tomorrow morning in Copenhagen, or is it Prague this week? You've finished all the work you planned to do on the flight and you lean back at full recline, nursing the cognac you allowed yourself after the meal. Next to you in 4B is not Henry Kissinger, as *The Economist* posited in a famous commercial a few years ago. But he does look like a fairly big-time executive – definitely board level. Never one to miss an opportunity to network, you turn to the big shot and introduce yourself. You shake hands. He's the marketing director of Global Huge Biz plc.

'What do you do?' he asks.

'I'm a consultant,' you reply.

Oh dear!

# THE ELEVATOR SPEECH

You must develop a brief outline of what you do that has signposts to positive action, should that be appropriate. And you should be able to deliver this in under 30 seconds – about 100 words. In the United States they call this the *elevator speech*. You never know whom you'll meet in the lift, so be prepared. Consultant Jack Carroll, principal of Mentor Associates, says an elevator speech should be 'a well-organized, delicious paragraph or two of compelling information about yourself'. He goes on to list these six basics for composing such a soundbite:

- What is your product/service/solution?
- Who is the customer it is intended for?
- What need or problem does it address?
- What does it do?
- How does it work and what are the benefits to me?
- What makes you different and better than others?

Go to Mentor Associates' Web site www.saleslinks.com for a nifty 'fill-in-the-blanks' template to create your own speech.

As Paul Villella of executive-recruiting firm Hire Strategy says, 'Thirty seconds is all the time you need to make a favourable first impression.' Here's mine (92 words):

We are a one-of-a-kind resource for advertisers, with a growing database of many thousands of English-language advertising slogans, covering all brand categories in all media. Every one of the top 20 ad agencies in London uses our services again and again to check prior or current use of slogans or to get up to speed on competition. So do many other top shops around the world. Our services are particularly useful in new-business pitches and in the creation of new campaigns. Our slogan? 'It pays to check.'

# TALK THE TALK

A lot of people have a problem describing what they do in ways that the customer will understand. They may be quite good at doing so in their own terms, but how well does it translate within their prospect's mind?

The problem is that we have a tendency to make assumptions about our customers – that they have a better understanding of our marketplace than they really do, or even that they might actually need us. Shift your definition of yourself or your products and services from an inward-looking point of view to one that respects the mindset of your customer.

For example, suppose you are in the business of analysing your clients' telephone bills to ensure that they are being properly charged. You also advise on the most appropriate phone-service packages, to optimize your clients' communications spend. So what is your business? Analysing phone bills or saving the client money and aggravation through your knowledge of the utilities marketplace? The first description imposes limits. Could you also analyse utilities costs, shipping costs, stationery purchases? Yes, but you'd have to redefine yourself. The second description permits more. It is more open-ended. It permits the client to ask if you can help in other areas – car fleet management, for instance.

Describing what you do should be results oriented rather than process related:

- You provide peace of mind in the development and implementation of local communications networks. You are not in the business of reviewing and specifying computer packages.

- You enable your clients' employees to be more oriented to delivering customer satisfaction. You are not in the business of designing and providing motivational training packages.

Here's a tangible example. Suppose you run a video-rental store. Are you in the business of renting videos? Are you a retailer? Are you in the entertainment business? Are you in the leisure business? Do people come to you because they want to rent a video or because they want to watch a movie?

A friend of mine, whose father owned a restaurant, opened a modest video-rental operation in a small parade of shops. But he went one better. He figured he was in the home-entertainment business, so he also set up a pizzeria in the back of the shop (see the lateral thinking coming out of the family heritage?). People tend to spend 10 or 15 minutes browsing through the film titles – just long enough to cook a pizza. So most customers come in, drop off their last film, go to the pizza counter, place their order, browse and select a film title, and then pick up their pizza. And of course the pricing reflects this: 'Large pizza, litre of Coke and a movie for £10.' Oh, and he also has a big cinema-style popcorn dispenser for those couch potatoes who really want to pretend they're going to the movies. Needless to say, he's very successful. He's shifted the spend per customer in many cases from maybe £2 a visit to £10 – a fivefold increase.

We shall cover more about building your credibility in Chapter 9.

# 3

# How to come across as a success

Procter & Gamble's Head and Shoulders anti-dandruff shampoo had a brilliant slogo a while back: *You only get one chance to make a first impression*. There's lot of truth in that statement, no matter what you do. So an important part of succeeding as an independent consultant means looking the *part* of someone who succeeds as an independent consultant. And acting as if you are a success. Speaking with a quaver in your voice, you know, and saying 'you know' at the end of every other clause in a sentence, you know, does not bespeak the ideal image, you know?

You need to look the part, speak the part and act the part. The least you can do is spend a bit of time in the dressing room before you go on stage, making sure you look the part. And you need to go over your lines. Presumably you've rehearsed these many times, so they should come almost automatically, but if you haven't, understand that rehearsal and role playing are essential. Far better you find out your embarrassing shortcomings and lack of answers in a non-threatening environment.

# LOOK THE PART

Dress according to the image of a successful person in your business. This may mean a three-piece suit, a set of overalls, a uniform or casual attire. But whatever it is, it needs to be clean and have that cared-for look.

If you deal with business people in offices, a classic suit is most appropriate. If you're behind the counter in a service business, perhaps a smart blazer or uniform jacket will work best. Think of the most successful businesses similar to your own, and think about how their best people look. Look no worse. In fact, look better. Your appearance might well be the first human manifestation of your business. Don't make it the last.

# SPEAK THE PART

Be knowledgeable about what you talk about. There's nothing that destroys your credibility faster than a blank stare and a quizzical look in answer to a simple question.

Avoid jargon. Unless you are talking to a person who is even more technically competent than yourself, using jargon, especially with an uninformed client, is showing off. Clients must not feel that you are putting them at a disadvantage. (Of course, there are whole industries based upon this sales technique...)

If you must use jargon, ask the customers if they understand what you mean when you do and explain the word or phrase if necessary.

# ACT THE PART

The only surprises you may allow your clients to experience are pleasant ones. Realize that every untoward experience is a step closer to 'no deal'. You want constantly to bring yourself into the realm of 'yes deal'. This means that their expectations should be constantly raised by good experiences, and each new experience should raise their expectations further.

It's as though you're always raising the bar. As they jump each hurdle towards satisfaction, they contemplate the next one as being at roughly the same level as the last one, but you discreetly raise it and, through your own interaction, let them experience the joy of jumping higher than they thought they could. Then they start thinking, 'This is different. This is better. I like this.'

Think back to the best two or three sales experiences you ever had as a *customer*. Reflect on how you felt afterwards. Was there not a feeling of satisfaction and reward beyond that of getting the product or service you wanted? Good salespeople love to be sold. Relish every good buying experience and see what you can learn from it. It makes sense even to write down a few thoughts to remind you in the future of the key points.

You'll surely find that your good feelings relate to having dealt with a person who understood your needs, understood the possible solutions and presented them in the most informative and convincing way.

What it boils down to is professionalism and a genuine interest in serving clients' needs. Ask yourself, 'Am I here because they are there, or are they there because I am here?' The answer will reveal all.

## BE ENTHUSIASTIC

Nobody likes a moaner. Enthusiasm is contagious, and can certainly help make the sale. A few years ago, I was in the bookshop at London's Gatwick Airport, on my way in to town. I usually took the opportunity to check on the display of my books on the Kogan Page spinner rack. Imagine my surprise and delight to find a woman browsing through my latest epic, *101 Ways to Generate Great Ideas*! I paused for a moment, and then went up to her and said, with a big smile, 'Now that's a *really good* book!' She looked up at me and said, 'It is?' 'Yes,' I replied. 'I wrote it, see?' and I showed her my business card. 'Oh, that's amazing!' she said. I replied, 'I'll tell you what, you buy it and I'll *sign* it for you!' 'OK,' she said. 'It'll make a good Christmas present for my husband.'

# BE OPTIMISTIC

Pessimism drags everyone down. When you are in a selling mode, pessimism can do nothing for you. Of course, you might be pessimistic and dealing with a customer who is *really* pessimistic, in which case you will come across relatively optimistic!

The issue is, you need to be conditioned to success, not failure. If you know you're not going to make the sale, your prediction will come true. If you know you *are* going to make it, it *might* come true.

# USE POSITIVE LANGUAGE

It's interesting how often we hear people using negative language to describe things. It goes back to 'Are you part of the problem or part of the solution?' See how these examples illustrate that, with positive versions beneath them:

- − 'We don't have it in stock' (= part of problem)
- + 'I can have one for you this afternoon; would you like it delivered?' (= part of solution)

- − 'The film has already started playing; you'll miss the opening' (= part of problem)
- + 'The next screening is at 9 o'clock' (= part of solution)

- − 'We close in five minutes' (= part of problem)
- + 'May I help you make your selection?' (= part of solution)

- − 'We don't take credit cards' (= part of problem)
- + 'If you prefer not to pay in cash, we could take a cheque' (= part of solution)

The problem is that it's natural for us to express difficulties in a negative way. So, as an exercise, pick five situations in your own business environment that are usually dealt with negatively and translate them into positive responses (use the part-of-problem/part-of-solution approach if it helps).

# IS WHAT YOU ARE DOING HELPING OR HINDERING YOUR SUCCESS?

There are people who make things happen. There are people things happen to. And there are people who wonder what happened. In which category are you or do you want to be?

Everything you do moves you in a certain direction. Even standing still moves you in a direction – maybe of failure. You need to make sure that, to the greatest possible extent, what you do moves you in the direction of success. Making an extra prospecting call moves you in the direction of success. Going home early, leaving the job to be picked up on next time you get to it does not.

Let's look at some other unfortunately all-too-familiar hindrances to success:

- keeping a client waiting;
- keeping a client waiting without any indication of how long before he or she'll be dealt with (worse);
- not answering the phone right away;
- not showing up at the appointed hour;
- not giving an appointed hour ('I'll try to get there as soon as I can – hopefully, it should be some time this week – or next, at the latest, if the rain holds off');
- not delivering as promised (the job is not done until you have come up with a *really good* excuse as to why the job is not done);
- delivering the wrong goods;

- delivering faulty goods;

- fixing faulty goods and they still don't work;

- providing hazardous (eg life-threatening) goods;

- delivering incomplete work;

- being unable to deliver on time, knowing this, but not advising the client of the expected delay.

What are some of your favourite client repellents?
   Now let's look at some helpful actions:

- dropping in to see a competitor's activity;

- trying your competitors' products or services;

- reading your competitors' advertising and brochures;

- reading a trade magazine on your business;

- going to a trade show about your business;

- talking to your colleagues about what clients are saying;

- talking to your clients;

- asking your clients for feedback on your products or services;

- delivering ahead of time;

- exceeding expectations;

- saying thank you for business.

What are some of your favourite customer attractors?

## IMPROVE TELEPHONE TECHNIQUES

Why is it that some people don't answer the phone right away when it's ringing? They look at it and glower. There seems to be an attitude that a phone call is not important. I was in Seeboard, the electrical retail store of south-eastern England. There were maybe three assistants in the shop. All were dealing with customers. The phone was ringing. And ringing. Forty to fifty rings. Nobody would answer it.

All it takes is a polite 'Excuse me, let me answer this.' If necessary, the caller can be called back. But just to let it ring is exactly how not to get more business. Letting the phone ring is being part of the problem. Answering it is being part of the solution. Personally, when I'm calling a retail establishment to get some information or place an order, I let it ring six times and then I hang up. Then I may call back later, but only if I wasn't able to get what I want elsewhere. I mean, what is the phone for?

Providing an answerphone or a 24-hour number is an obvious step in the right direction of good customer service. But another very important aspect is returning the phone call. I'm amazed at how often people don't return phone calls. Bill collectors I can understand suffering this problem. But somebody offering services? The winners are, and always will be, those who handle their telephones professionally and thoughtfully.

Putting someone on hold should not mean seemingly everlasting banishment. Even if you have (ugh!) 'music on hold', the holdee should be advised at least every *30 seconds* of their status.

# RECOGNIZE THE IMPORTANCE OF TRAINING

Airline pilots keep on training. Doctors keep on training. So what about you? You're reading this book, and you're this far into it, so I guess you recognize it. And I'll say it anyway. Don't fall behind. Go to seminars, trade shows, exhibitions. Read the trade press. Read books like this. Listen to motivational tapes. Network, network, network. Constantly upgrade your skills and knowledge. There's nothing like a good training session to shake the cobwebs out.

# 4

# How to distinguish yourself

## HOW ARE YOU POSITIONED IN YOUR PROSPECTS' MINDS?

If you're just starting out, you may be surprised to know that you are already positioned in your prospects' minds. Your positioning may be 'Who?', but it's a positioning, nevertheless. You are then lodged with the group headed 'Never heard of them.' Or it may be 'Oh yes, I've heard of them – what is it they do again?' You want to be in the rarefied atmosphere of total trust and reliance: 'They're the greatest – absolutely top-rate.' You can only get there by earning it.

You can only earn it by enabling your contacts to experience what you have to offer first-hand. A succession of positive experiences will build increasing trust and a sense of your own reliability. Negative experiences will be very destructive. People tend to share negative experiences 10 times as much as they share positive experiences.

Who controls your positioning? You? And if not you, who? And what are you doing about it?

The key point is that you're positioned differently with different members of your audience. With your best client, your positioning is quite different from that with someone whose bag of groceries you just scattered when you bumped into that person on the street.

Recognizing where you stand with your different targets will help you move yourself up the positioning ladder with each of them to a position of total trust and reliance. We'll look at this subject a little closer in Chapter 11.

And don't forget that your USP must be part of your positioning. That's why so many companies put a slogan with their logo – I call it a slogo. Here are three of my favourites:

- *Taste. Not waist.*
  Weight Watchers Frozen Meals

- *Getting there is half the fun.*
  Cunard Steamship Lines

- *When it absolutely, positively, has to be there overnight.*
  Federal Express

## WHAT SHOULD BE YOUR SLOGO?

Some people call slogos straplines. If they're in a TV commercial, they're known as endlines. In the United States, they're called taglines; in Germany, they're claims; in the Netherlands, they're pay-offs; in France, they're signatures. They form part of the heritage of the brand. Some of them are so famous and well known they immediately conjure up an image of the brand. Try these. What are their brands?

- *Don't leave home without it.*
  American Express or Visa?

- *The pause that refreshes.*
  Coke or Pepsi?

- *The best to you each morning.*
  Maxwell House or Kellogg's?

- *We try harder.*
  Avis or Budget?

- *Just do it.*
  Reebok or Nike?

- *The ultimate driving experience.*
  BMW or Porsche?

I'll bet you got 'em all right (the answers are aababa).

A good slogo should state a benefit and be relevant to the brand. You should be able to ask for the brand by using the slogo.

Good examples:

- *The antidote for civilization.*
  Club Med

- *The best way of expressing your intelligence.*
  Zenith Data Systems

- *As sure as taking it there yourself.*
  United Parcel Service

- *We'll do the homework.*
  Tricity Bendix

- *Finger-lickin' good!*
  KFC

A poor slogo may not work for various reasons – usually because the line sounds like the brand manager talking to his or her peers. Or because the line is simply meaningless or irrelevant. Who cares? Does this mean I should use it? Try these gems:

- *All it leaves behind is other non-bios.*
  Fairy Ultra Detergent

- *Britain's second largest international scheduled airline.*
  Air Europe

- *A company called TRW.*
  TRW

Then again, whose lines are these, anyway?

- The natural choice.

- Where people make the difference.

- Simply the best.

- It's about time.

- Taste the difference.

The answer is 'anybody's'. Each of those lines is used by about 50 different brands. Your guess is as good as mine as to which. It's six of one and half a dozen of the other. You pays your money and you takes your choice.

## HOW TO WRITE A SLOGO

You may say, 'I'm not creative enough to write a slogo.' But I say you are! You just have to understand the process. What you need is a great new idea. And where do they come from? Great old ideas! There is no such thing as a new idea created from a vacuum. All new ideas are based on old ideas.

Make a list of slogos you like – about 50 of them. These are the old ideas you will use for inspiration:

- Some should be commands:
  *Stay in touch.*

- Some should be rhetorical wisdom:
  *It's good to talk.*

- Some should be catchy:
  *It's for yoo-hoo.*

- Some should be rhymes:
  *Don't just book it, Thomas Cook it.*

- Some should be puns:
  *It's how the smooth take the rough.*

- Some should be strategic:
  *Engineering tomorrow's world.*

- Some should be three punchy words:
  *Quality. Value. Service.*

- Or even the fashionable one-word approach:
  *Invent.*

There are plenty of other styles, but you get the idea.

Having assembled a list of favourite lines, go through the exercise of rewriting them to suit your business. If you are an Internet Web site consultant, you might turn *Quality. Value. Service* into *Understanding. Creativity. Commitment.* You might rewrite *It's how the smooth take the rough* into *It's how surfers learn new tricks.*

You should now have about 50 new lines. Then simply reduce them to a short list of about 10 and massage these until you get two or three winners. Review these with your friends or colleagues and pick one. Make sure it's not in use by an arch-rival and you're there! The quintessence of your positioning is yours. By the way, my slogo is now *It pays to check.* Before that it was *Check. Create. Inspire.*

We'll revisit the subject of positioning, as it applies to building relationships, in Chapter 11, after we've reviewed some other aspects of the task.

## SHOULD YOU HAVE A MISSION STATEMENT?

A mission statement is the driver of many leading enterprises – an affirmation of their philosophy and direction. It is developed by a business or organization to focus people on what the entity is about, where they are going and how they intend to get there.

Developing your own mission statement can be a useful exercise. It should contain a statement of your vision and values. It should express what makes you tick and where you stand. It could be an amplification of your slogo. As such it can be very helpful in focusing you on what you do.

# 5

# How to know your customer

Having a good understanding of your client or prospect is a key success factor in your role as an independent consultant. You need a clear idea of who you would like your customer to be, how the customer thinks about your area of interest and what the customer wants. So you need to define your customers and prospects. Start here:

- What industries?
- What locations?
- What type of organization?
- What size?
- What specific organizations?
- What areas of interest within the organization?
- What job titles?
- What names?

In my success plan in Chapter 1, I defined my customers and prospects as people responsible for the development of advertising:

- at ad agencies, eg J Walter Thompson, Leo Burnett;

- at multi-brand organizations that advertise, eg Unilever, Procter & Gamble, General Motors;

- located principally in the United States, the United Kingdom and other parts of the English-speaking world;

- in global organizations based anywhere that use English as their main operating language, eg ABB, Philips, Siemens.

## HOW TO FIND THEM

You need to know how you can identify these people. These methods work:

- personal networking;

- Web sites;

- directories;

- professional organizations/trade associations;

- mailing lists;

- news items;

- press releases;

- trade shows and exhibitions.

## WHO DO YOU WANT YOUR CUSTOMERS TO BE?

In the best of all possible worlds, whom would you *like* to be working with? Remember Basil Fawlty in *Fawlty Towers*, getting so excited because he thought he had a lord as guest at his hotel? ('I sign my name Melbury because I am *Lord* Melbury.') No more riffraff for him! Of course, it turned out in the end that Melbury was a conman.

Does it matter who your customers should be? Isn't one person's money as good as another's? Of course. But it may be that one type of customer is better for you because those customers are more knowledgeable and you don't have to spend so much time explaining things. Or they have deeper pockets and might be easier to sell to. Or they have other needs as well that you can also fill. So take a few moments to think about who your ideal customer is. And is not...

# WHOM DON'T YOU WANT AS CUSTOMERS?

Obviously you don't want time wasters and tyre kickers. When I was a stockbroker in Toronto, I found that one kind of client I didn't want was the kind with a large investment portfolio – 10,000 shares of International Nickel, 1,000 IBM, that sort of thing – and all he would do was talk about how he might buy 10,000 more Nickel, or sell the IBM and buy Digital, but he never *did* anything! Since my living was based on transactions, this was dire. I identified this type of client as a stock teaser.

You don't want people who spend hours getting your advice and then go off and buy somewhere else. Or people who buy and then come back some months later and want to return the goods, now worn, because they're not satisfactory. Or people who ask you to submit a proposal on speculation, spend hours in meetings with you and then hire someone else (whom they were going to use anyway – they were just fishing for some free thinking).

Well, surely you know whom you don't want to deal with? Make a list. Here are some types you may prefer not to have as customers:

- people who want you to work for nothing on the understanding that you will get lots of well-paid business as soon as the product or service is launched;

- people who take too long to pay their bills;

- people who constantly argue about your pricing, always holding out for a discount, and then take too long to pay their bills;

- people who ask for a detailed, tailored presentation of your ideas with little prospect of action (some prospects are required to get three bids on a project – you may just be 'bid fodder');

- people who want you to compromise your standards.

I got a call from a man who had heard that I was a writer. He invited me over to his sumptuous country estate to brief me on a script he needed. It turned out that he had one of those £1-per-minute telephone lines and he wanted a script for a come-on about his course on how to become a private detective. He had been running ads for this in the *Sun*, and was making a lot of money on putting out profligate promises to poor penniless punters. But he wanted it lengthened so as to increase the take per call. I asked to see the course and he said it was 'in development'. I bid him a fast farewell and escaped.

## What is your customer interface?

On what basis do you work with your customers? Do they deal with you face to face, or over the phone? Or by mail or e-mail? Do they come to you or do you go to them? Do you have to do a lot of travelling? Or do they?

# WHO IS YOUR DREAM CUSTOMER?

As an exercise, imagine you receive an e-mail offering you your absolutely best, most magnificent, ideal, superb, appropriate project, assignment or piece of business. You couldn't ask for anything better!

Who is the e-mail from? What is the deal? What do you have to do to make it really happen? What are the barriers? So what are you going to do about it?

This exercise can produce some amazing results for you. If you give yourself permission to get the ideal kind of project or piece of business, you can find new opportunities opening up that you may have pooh-poohed as being unachievable. Yet anything is achievable. All you have to do is identify the goal, establish what you have to do to get there and do it.

An awful lot of what gets done gets done because somebody said, 'Let's do it.' President Kennedy set the goal of putting a man on the moon by the end of the 1960s. It was done. Rupert Murdoch decided to build a new TV network, came up with the ways to get around restrictive and protective legislation, and did it with Sky TV. Fred Smith avowed that the best way to move millions of packages around the United States was by a hub-and-spoke system using his own aircraft, where everything was flown to Memphis, sorted and then flown to its destination. The result was Federal Express, now the model for all other courier services.

So identify the result you want to achieve, ask the magic question 'What do we have to do to get there?' and do it.

## WHAT DO YOUR PROSPECTS THINK OR KNOW ABOUT YOUR AREA OF INTEREST?

Are your prospects experienced in your area of expertise? Or are they uninformed and bewildered? For example, if you write and design brochures, you can expect most of your prospects to have a pretty good idea of what's involved. They know about layouts and illustrations, typography and printing, paper quality and distribution. So your role is less advisory and more executional. You can't charge a hell of a lot for this kind of non-specialized work.

But perhaps you consult in the area of wireless intranet optical broadband digital packet-switched satellite-backed LAN multimedia throughput connection hardware firewalls. Now your prospects are probably much more in the dark. Your role here is much more consultative. Your contribution is more valuable, and you can charge accordingly.

Your prospect's lack of knowledge about a subject, and your superior breadth and depth of experience impact your marketability and what you can charge. Are you a £10-an-hour menial, or do you get £1,000 per day? Some whiz-kids can charge £10,000 a day and more. Part of this may be due to reputation, part due to deliverable results.

It is your job as an independent consultant to be aware of knowledge and experience levels within your marketplace. You find out by immersing yourself in the trade press, personal networking and market research. There is a lot of information out there, just waiting to be useful for you. You can search the Internet (the best search engine, bar none, is Google, www.google.com).

Or go to libraries and search through:

- directories;

- reference books;

- encyclopedias;

- almanacs;

- atlases;

- dictionaries;

- biographies;

- newspapers;

- magazines.

The librarian will help you, and can do computer and microfiche searches for you to identify books on particular subjects. There are also useful specialist libraries. Ten years ago, I wrote, produced and directed a video called *Wheels – The Joy of Cars*, which was an assembly of a variety of interesting footage from newsreels and other film archives over the years. One bit featured the Royal Automobile Club (RAC) vintage-car London-to-Brighton rally of about 20 years earlier. I wanted to identify the various ancient vehicles, and all I had to go on was their rally number and a vague description (red, open top, two seats). I telephoned the RAC library. The librarian pulled out the original rally programme, I read him the cars' numbers and I soon had the identifications I needed.

Or maybe you do some original research of your own. This can help you drive your whole programme. When I was working on a marketing assignment for Mooney Aircraft of Kerrville, Texas, we wanted to know more about the Mooney customer. Mooney made exotic high-performance single-engine four-seater private planes. I did a mailing to all Mooney owners to find out a whole raft of things – why they bought the aeroplane (efficiency, performance), did they intend to buy another Mooney (yes), what sort of flying they did (long trips, short trips, business, holidays, training), age groups, occupations – even things like ownership of videocassette recorders (VCRs). In those days, the level of VCR ownership in the United States was about 25 per cent. I surmised that Mooney owners, being techies and gadget freaks, would be more likely to own VCRs than plain non-plane folks. Correct: penetration was closer to 50 per cent. One idea was to use video to build the relationship with Mooney owners. I wanted eventually to put the owner's manual and some advanced training material on video.

We started with a film called *The Mooney Experience*. This was designed to make a Mooney owner salivate, and want desperately to show it to his (or her) friends. It featured some beautiful footage that demonstrated the core concept of the Mooney – its aerodynamic efficiency.

We sold 600 copies of this tape to Mooney owners through the mail and invited them to show it to their friends and bring potential customers into the showrooms. We promised them a $1,000 bounty if a plane was sold as a result. Three new Mooneys (over $360,000 worth of aeroplanes – this was 1982!) thus moved out of the hangars in the next couple of months. All from a little research carried out to confirm an idea.

# FOCUS GROUPS

Focus groups involve getting groups of people together in a controlled environment and conducting an in-depth inquiry into your challenge. This process is quite expensive, compared to making a few phone calls or sending out questionnaires, but if it is done properly it's well worth while.

Typically, the focus group is conducted by a specialist company. They may even have specially designed premises to do the job. I went to one in my Merrill Lynch days when we were designing a new financial service, and we had 10 investors in a room for four hours. They didn't know who the client was. We were watching from behind one-way glass, and the whole process was videotaped. Very eerie and very helpful.

You can use a focus group to identify perceived problems with your approach. You can show them your advertising or your commercial, or a write-up of the service, or a mock-up of the product. If it's skilfully handled, you can get a lot of information and a better understanding of your customer very quickly. By holding several focus groups with different types of people – heavy users, light users, non-users, men, women, doctors, airline pilots, mothers, mothers with teenage daughters, teenagers, etc – you can focus on the information you need to develop. You can also conduct the groups regionally: north, south, urban, rural, seaside, inland, French, German, multinational and so on.

The secret of good focus groups is to have the right people in the group (the focus group firm *must* know how to find these) and have it run by an experienced facilitator who really understands what you want to achieve. Many words spoken by participants in a focus group have ended up as great advertising copy. You can't make up the kind of stuff you get from a focus group. It's too real.

Holding a focus group is a good way to identify or confirm a core problem that needs solving.

# 6

# How to promote what you do

In the early days of your career, you don't have much to go on. You start with an education, some job experience and a few lucky breaks. Merge in good personal presentation and communication skills, and you're on your way. Start delivering, and you'll make a name for yourself. Then people will recommend you to their friends and you will become more successful.

The up-front problem is, it's a very competitive world out there, and there are a lot of other people trying to get at the same bones that you want to chew on. In Chapter 2 we discussed the need to differentiate yourself, to find something unique about what you do. Next you must find a good way to get that message in front of the right people. Here are some ideas.

## HAVE YOUR OWN WEB SITE

Your own Web site on the Internet can be the most important tool in your inventory of promotional devices. It can have all the power and appetite-appeal of a brochure, with none of the printing and distribution costs. If it's well designed, you can lead your prospects down the paths you want them to take, to the destination of your choosing. You can initiate action on the spot. You can deal all over the world.

But your Web site has to be done well for it to be effective. My advice, having tried doing it myself, is to employ a skilled Web-site designer. My Web site went through three DIY incarnations, ultimately with good navigation but an appallingly unappealing look, before I finally got smart and hired some help.

This is how it feels being involved with the Internet and having your own decent Web site for your business:

- It's like getting a terrific new job involving worldwide, all-expenses-paid travel – with a visa and a free pass to strange new lands you may have never visited before, as well as to your old familiar haunts.

- It's like having membership in an array of exclusive clubs addressing all your special interests, expanding your personal network hugely.

- It's like being a child, thrilling at the new learning and capabilities constantly pouring in.

- It's like having your own showroom that you can set up in clients' offices in a few seconds, the better to discuss how they can benefit from your offering.

## Planning mandatory

Yes, it will take planning – scheme out as much of your site as you can before you start putting it together. Every hour of real planning time will save you at least one day undoing mistakes and rethinking things later.

## Questions to answer

### How do you want your site to look and feel?

From this moment on, as you surf the Web, include one more consideration. Does this site I'm looking at really knock me out? Is there something here I could emulate? Is this the kind of look I want? If you say yes, bookmark the site and make a file of sites you like. Do it for sites you don't like, as well. This will give you some benchmarks to work with when you start developing your own site.

## What is the purpose of your site?

This is what I came up with for mine:

- to raise awareness of my work among my audiences;
- to provide a reason to call/e-mail clients and prospects;
- to be a basis for publicity;
- to open the door to new business;
- to be easily searched for and *found*, using obvious keywords, by all the main search engines (Google, Yahoo!, AltaVista, Lycos, etc);
- to provide a mechanism for doing business;
- to identify and locate allies and competitors;
- to link to and from allies (adds to credibility);
- to enable satisfied customers to show off their knowledge by introducing their colleagues to my services via the Web site;
- to encourage feedback on my work;
- to encourage frequent return visits to the Web site in order to build confidence in what I do.

## Whom are you aiming at?

- Defined, known, named clients and prospects?
- Categories of people (airline pilots, lawyers, gardeners...)?
- The general public?

- People who don't have computers and have never used the Internet?

- Or whom?

### What would you like as your domain name?

That's the core address point in your URL (Uniform Resource Locator – the Web-site address). My domain is adslogans.co.uk, but adslogans.com had already gone when I started being serious (it's still perennially 'under construction'). You can reserve an available name in advance if needed by paying a modest fee – check with your Internet service provider (ISP).

# DOS AND DON'TS OF WEB SITE WIZARDRY

- Do proofread your text for typos, grammar and spelling. It's amzaing how many its/it's your/you're there/their/they're mistskes there are.

- Do have your contact details readily available on your home page, including a name, e-mail and postal addresses, phone and fax numbers.

- Do make it easy to navigate by putting buttons to other pages on every page – top and bottom.

- Do include hyperlinks within your text – underlined key words that can be clicked on for transportation to more detail on that subject.

- Do have a links page giving connections to other relevant sites – but have the link open up on a new page so you are still there underneath for a quick return.

- Do make quantity and size of pictures small to keep loading time short.

- Do keep your site up to date – especially if you mention dates. To see 'Coming Monday 2 November!' is a real turn-off on Friday 8 March 2002, especially when you realize that the Monday 2 November reference was in 1998!

- Do include items that will encourage repeat visits. I have a slogan quiz called 'What's My Brand?' that changes every week.

- Don't have a long, complicated animation sequence at the beginning of your site that takes two minutes to load and ends up saying 'Welcome to our site! To enter, click HERE.' One personal Web site I saw had a full-length photo of the site-owner, of which the top 3 inches was sky, followed by 1 inch of hair, 2 inches of face and so on. It took so long to load that my screensaver came on! Give us a break, folks! Long, boring downloads are seldom finished – the surfer moves on.

- Don't lay out any text wider than 300 pixels, unless you want it to be hard to read. Notice how magazines and newspapers use narrow text columns.

- Don't display widely set text on the right side of the screen or you'll force readers with smaller screens to scroll left and right every line, which is torture.

- Don't take readers to the bottom of a page without giving them somewhere to go next. If it's a long story, have 'NEXT' and 'PREVIOUS' buttons at the page top and bottom and 'TOP' buttons at the bottom of every screen display.

Since I've had my Web site, I have done business with clients in Australia, Austria, Brazil, Canada, Croatia, Denmark, Finland, France, Georgia, Germany, India, Ireland, Israel, Italy, Japan, Korea, the Netherlands, Poland, Singapore, South Africa, Spain, Switzerland, the United Arab Emirates and the United States, and the list is growing day by day. Last year, 25 per cent of my business came from outside the United Kingdom, mostly attributable to my Web site.

One of the most useful gadgets on my site is a 'call me now' phone button. If visitors want to talk to me *now*, they click the phone button, which is on just about every page, enter their name, phone number and e-mail address on the screen, and click the 'call me' button. Through the miracle of technology, I immediately receive a phone call, backed up by an e-mail, advising me of the request and details. 'If you want to place the call, press 1.' I do so and the phone starts ringing at the visitor's location. Forty seconds have elapsed. The visitor is always most impressed at the speed of the connection and it goes a long way to building my credibility. The first time it was used, I got a call request from the United States and in 10 minutes of conversation (including a guided tour of my Web site) I obtained a $400 order. Not bad!

## BE FOUND ON SEARCH ENGINES

The most important aspect of having a Web site is how well you show up on search engines. There are services you can subscribe to that will advise on this and will handle submissions to hundreds of search engines for you.

Ideally when someone is looking for Web sites about what you do, they should see yours listed in the top 10 findings. The secret is to identify appropriate keywords and key phrases that people would be most likely to use when seeking the likes of you. Then you have to make sure those words appear on your home page in a natural way. (Many search engines are programmed to ignore assemblies of keywords repeated over and over, eg slogans slogans slogans slogans slogans slogans.)

Here is the original introductory text from my own Web site:

ADSlogans Unlimited is a unique resource for advertisers and marketers. We have built a growing database of many thousands of advertising slogans/straplines/taglines/endlines/claims.

These lines have appeared mostly in the UK and USA, during the last ten-plus years. The resource also includes many historical lines and covers all brand categories in all media.

We provide advertising agencies and marketing organizations with a variety of customized reports about slogans. All of the top-twenty ad agencies in London use our services to check prior or current use of slogans. So do many other top shops around the world.

After some advice from a search-engine optimization company, I changed it to the following. Just about every relevant search keyword is now in the text:

ADSlogans Unlimited, home of the Advertising Slogan Hall of Fame, runs the world's most comprehensive advertising slogans database archive. A unique global resource for advertisers and ad agencies, comprising many thousands of English-language commercial advertising slogans, business, company, product or brand marketing slogans, taglines or tag lines, claims, straplines, theme lines, endlines, payoffs, signatures, base lines, slogos (the slogan by the logo) and catchphrases. These are often unregistered, and hard to find in standard trademark registers or directories.

By subscribing to a tracking service that monitors your site, you can, on demand, see how the visitors to your site got there, plus other important details.

For example, my tracker showed that the two most prevalent search phrases used to find us were 'Advertising Slogans' (46 per cent of search terms used) and 'Advertising Taglines' (18 per cent). It showed that the top five search engines for getting people on to our site were:

| | |
|---|---|
| Yahoo! | 51 per cent of all referrals |
| Google | 40 per cent |
| Lycos | 3 per cent |
| Ask Jeeves | 3 per cent |
| Dog Pile | 2 per cent |

I then searched these top five engines, using the two most prevalent phrases, to see where we came on the list of findings. Searches for the phrase 'Advertising Slogans' put us in these positions:

| Lycos | 2nd on the list |
| Ask Jeeves | 2nd |
| Yahoo! | 5th |
| Google | 5th |
| Dog Pile | 12th |

Searches for the phrase 'Advertising Taglines' put us in these positions:

| Lycos | 2nd on the list |
| Yahoo! | 2nd |
| Google | 3rd |
| Ask Jeeves | 4th |
| Dog Pile | 10th |

You can see that monitoring this kind of information can drive you into refining your Web site to achieve maximum results.

# GET LINKED

Many Web sites carry a 'Useful Links' section. Surf away, looking for appropriate ones that will carry a link to your site, usually at no cost. (You may be asked to provide a reciprocal link from your site back to them.) An example is a trade association or business directory (some of these now charge a fee). This kind of link will provide the visitor to the other site with the ability to come to your site with one simple click. The most productive such link that I have is from the University of Texas Advertising World directory, which produced 380 click-throughs to my site just last month. Bear in mind there's an implied endorsement of you from the other site.

When you're on the site that you want to link to you, look for a button or hypertext that says something like 'Want us to link to you?' or 'Submit URL' and follow their instructions.

# RISE ABOVE THE NOISE

We are all inundated with communications. Beyond the Internet, how can you make your message work – taking you above the general background noise? I used to write television scripts, and I needed to communicate with people in TV production companies. I devised a mailing piece that resembled a storyboard – the kind of depiction of a TV script that tells the story in a series of frames. I even called it a storyboard (see Figure 6.1).

It produced a quarter of my total revenue in the first year I used it. Not only was the communication original, it was memorable. I could say on the phone, 'I'm the chap that sent you a CV that looks like a storyboard' – instant recall! One producer who ended up giving me a lot of work said, on my first phone call to him, 'I've got it right here and I want to meet you!'

# DO A MAILING – BUT MAKE IT RELEVANT

A little reminder in the mail never did any harm. You have a list of your clients and prospects? It's clean and up to date, with no duplications or silliness (dead people/fired people/gross errors)? When did you last do a general mailing to them? If it's over six months ago, maybe it's time to do another. What will you mail? Tell them some news about you, but make it relevant to their needs.

# ASK FOR A REPLY

One of my most successful mailing pieces includes a postcard with a *postage stamp* on it (not a reply-paid card). It also contains a duplicate of the mailing label I used on the outside envelope. This invites them to ask me to call, to explain something about what I've sent them or to tell me they're not interested. I get about a 15 per cent response.

## This is the storyboard of a freelance video writer, producer, director who is available now for challenging projects

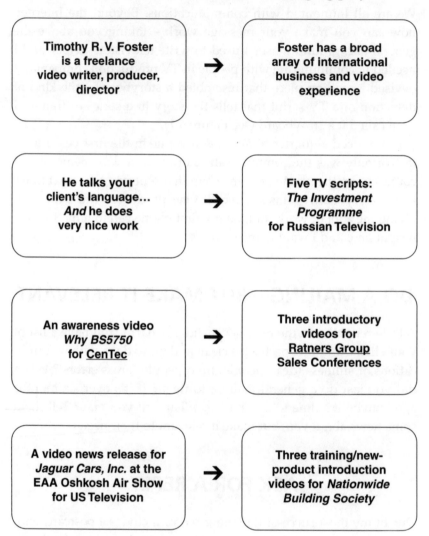

**Figure 6.1**  *Mailing piece designed to resemble a storyboard*

# RUN AN ADVERTISEMENT – BUT GET IT RIGHT

An advertisement can be costly unless you get it exactly right. I ran a quarter-page ad for a video I produced – *Your Guide to Antique Shopping in Britain* – in the special antiques issue of *Country Life*, and sold three tapes. When I was head of advertising for Merrill Lynch in Toronto, we ran a double-page ad in the *Globe and Mail* with a coupon offering any of 29 different pieces of investment information, and received hundreds of replies, opening dozens of accounts. And an analysis of the 29 boxes that had to be ticked to receive the appropriate information told us a lot about what investors' interests and concerns were at that time.

'Only half of my advertising is effective,' said one corporate ad biggie. 'The trouble is, I don't know which half!' My advice is, unless you can afford to run regular advertising with a consistent message, you'll find other techniques more effective. One little ad won't do.

# CREATE A NEWSLETTER

Do you have enough activity to warrant a regular newsletter? One of my suppliers, a computer dealer, sends me one, and as a result I've visited their showroom five times. So far, I've spent over £500 there in three months. I've hired their services as a consultant in developing some software, and I've had some equipment repaired. We have a *relationship*. And I'm looking lustfully at the new models that have recently been introduced.

Now, with e-mail, you can whiz off your newsletter in no time and distribute it, complete with hyperlinks to your Web site, at no cost.

# PLACE AN ARTICLE ABOUT WHAT YOU DO

Perhaps you have an interesting enough story for an appropriate publication. When I made the video *Your Guide to Antique Shopping in Britain*, I got myself interviewed by the editor of *World of Antiques*. This ended up as a two-page article in the magazine. It was all about why I did it, and went into the philosophy behind the programme. Then the story became part of the sales presentation, to show the retailers the coverage we were getting. Later I placed an article in *Retirement Living*, which was basically a modification of the video's script. We offered the tape in a sidebar and sold dozens.

# GET REVIEWS OF WHAT YOU DO

Somebody does something, and there's always somebody else to pass an opinion. If you're in the right sort of field, seek out opportunities for people to review your activities – assuming you're proud of them! In my case, a review of one of my books, *The Aircraft Owner's Handbook*, became part of my advertising programme. *Aviation Consumer* – a sort of US private pilot's *Which?* magazine – reviewed it in these words: 'With this book, the Library of Congress can close the doors to the general aviation stacks, because it's all there in eight vast codices unlike anything we've ever seen.' *Art and Auction*, a US magazine, said of the antiques video, 'A must for anyone who wants to try their hand at treasure hunting in the UK... this video cassette is required watching.' *That* went on the wrapper.

But maybe you don't write books or make videos. So what kind of review can you get? Look at the trade press for your industry. Don't they review products? *Flying* magazine reviews aeroplanes and all the stuff that goes with them. Car mags review cars. Camera mags review cameras. *Campaign* reviews advertising. *PR Week* reviews PR campaigns. What do you do that can earn a review?

Then you make the reviews part of your programme. They go on your Web site, into your mailings, into your handouts, whatever.

# DEVELOP A BROCHURE

A brochure is designed to represent the product or service until it has been acquired or employed. It is there to help reinforce or replace personal experience. It needs to describe the *benefits* in glowing terms, creating desire. It should impart some of the same feelings as the real thing in an appetizing way. It should ring of the same quality as the end product. (Not like the one I saw from a desktop publishing agency offering 'Word Procesing'.) It should inform. It should be a reference point (including things like technical specifications, dimensions, Web site URL, addresses, phone and fax numbers and so on). When your prospect or client wants action, the brochure should prompt a successful conclusion (business!). It should then become a hand-me-down, wending its way as an unsolicited testimonial into the arms of one of your clients' friends, along with a recommendation to use you or what you do.

# DO A PRESS RELEASE

Got something new to report? Will your trade press cover it? Then maybe a press release is the answer. No more than two or three pages of double-spaced typing, with a compelling headline and introduction, accompanied perhaps by a photo. Make sure the photo has a caption, and that the press release has a contact point (names, phone and fax numbers, e-mail address). Your objective is to establish a basis for further contact. Maybe the release will prompt a call from the publication asking for more information.

However, people who get press releases get perhaps 20 or more a day. So don't expect yours to be read all the way through in the first instance. First, you've got to get their attention! Your headline and the opening paragraph are the most important words on the paper.

Think about what kind of story the publication is looking for. Does your release sing this out? It has to.

# CREATE A PRESS KIT

In an attractive folder, gather a variety of implements describing your act. A copy of your brochure. The latest press releases (make sure the old, out-of-date ones are pulled). Reprints of articles. Photos. Diagrams, drawings, charts. Anything that brings your story to life and that can be a reference for an inquisitive journalist. Hand it out to appropriate members of the press. The strategy is to use the press as influencers of your real audience, your clients and prospects.

# DO A FILOFAX INSERT

Have you noticed that a lot of your business contacts use Filofaxes? Then why not produce a page or two that will fit in their Filofax giving useful information about you and your industry? When I was a video producer, I created a reference page on which the holder could enter the names and numbers of freelance video crew people. My name and numbers were prominently displayed under the headings 'Writers', 'Producers' and 'Directors'. On the back I put the phone numbers of key TV industry organizations, so it would be even more helpful to users.

# CREATE A CALENDAR OR DESKTOP ITEM

Amazingly enough, people still need calendars. The calendar industry knows this and offers all sorts of solutions. Can you produce one that's relevant to you and that acts as a constant reminder?

In connection with my advertising slogan business, I send out a calendar every year. It is called 'Advertising Memories' and is published by the History of Advertising Trust. It features old ads, to which I have applied a think bubble on each that says 'Oh gosh! I hope they check with ADSlogans...' The think bubble was a pressure-sensitive oval label I had printed by Viking Direct.

What do people need on their desks that could have your name and number on it? The promotional products people await your call. Coffee cups? Coasters? Calculators? Pens and pencils? Paper clip dispensers? Paperweights? Executive-decision-maker spinners? There's got to be something relevant to what you do that would work effectively.

## GET LISTED IN TRADE DIRECTORIES

I'm amazed at how effective listings in trade directories can be. Newcomers and outsiders often use directories as their primary reference when they seek a solution to a problem. I got a nice piece of business once because I was in the *Broadcast Production Guide.* My listing produced the speaking engagement that has culminated in this book. The *Yellow Pages* or *Thomson Directory* can be important, too. But make sure they list it right. Years ago there was a coffee bar in Toronto called The Bohemian Embassy. You got it – you had to look it up in the *Yellow Pages* under 'Embassies and Consulates'.

## JOIN A RELEVANT CLUB

Where do your kind of business people hang out? Maybe there's a club or other establishment (pub? restaurant? bar?) where the clan gathers. Regular attendance may be hazardous to your health, but it can also help oil the way to further, more businesslike meetings.

## JOIN A RELEVANT TRADE ASSOCIATION

For people in video production, it's the International Visual Communications Association. You get a listing in their directory, you get a certificate, you get membership benefits and a magazine, and you get to attend meetings where you can be a speaker and network to your heart's content. Consider standing as an officer. It could give you more clout.

# BE SOMEONE IN THE COMMUNITY

There are plenty of community activities that could make use of your services. When I lived in the United States, I became the PR adviser to a community action group that was fighting a nasty sewage-treatment plant proposal (nasty for us – it was to be upwind of our back yards!). Each week I attended meetings with the local community leaders, expanding my personal network the while. (We won, too.)

# BE FAMOUS FOR SOMETHING ELSE

What happens to old boxing champions in the United States? They become greeters at Caesar's Palace in Las Vegas. Retired sports stars become car/insurance salespeople or stockbrokers. Record-breaking runners become newsreaders. Is there something in your past you can cash in on? Were you a child star? Or in your present? Are you an ace amateur athlete? What notoriety have you that you can put to use?

Many years ago, in what seems like a previous incarnation, I was the author of the only Canadian pilot's instrument rating training course. I became very well known in Canadian aeronautical circles. Then I joined Merrill Lynch as a stockbroker. Fresh out of the seven-month training programme, I sent out my first prospect mailing to a list of pilots. My letter started out 'Dear Fellow Pilot: You may know me as the author of...' Naturally, the mailing included a reply-paid folder to engender response. Soon I received my first one back in the mail. With shaking hands I opened it. Here is what was written inside: 'It is only because you are a fellow pilot that I have chosen to break these long years of silence, (signed) Amelia Earhart.' And she didn't even give me her address!

# WRITE A BOOK

I do a stand-up piece at seminars called 'Write a book about what you do.' It is absolutely the best way to become an acknowledged leader in your area whom people seek out for advice!

## Check the existing literature

Look at your line of business. What books are there out there now on the subject? Who publishes them? You should have a reasonable awareness of this, but if you don't, visit a good library. Go to a couple of good bookshops and check out the scene. On the Web, go to www.amazon.co.uk, pick a keyword that would be in the title and search books of that ilk.

## Checklist for writing a book

To start, answer these questions:

- What is my objective?
- What is the working title?
- What is the subtitle?
- What is the book about?
- Who will buy it?
- What needs does it fill?
- What does the author bring to the party?
- What is the format (hardcover, paperback, etc)?
- Who should publish it?

Assuming you can answer these, start working. Write the table of contents. Write single-paragraph descriptions of each chapter, and write at least one chapter.

## Selling your book

Forget agents. They are mostly *useless* for this kind of work. I've never had an agent able to sell a trade book on my behalf. Most of them don't even want to look at what you do, because they're 'too busy'. Yet I've sold over 20 books on my own, working directly with publishers.

So write to your target publisher. If you don't know whom to contact, telephone and ask for the name of the person to write to, and send a one-page descriptive letter, with this information:

- the proposed title;
- the target audience;
- the rationale/need for the book;
- the chapter headings;
- how many pages you expect it to be;
- the style – paperback, coffee-table, etc;
- how many illustrations;
- when and how you can deliver it (disk, paper, etc);
- your price ideas;
- your timetable;
- your credentials as an author – CV, copies of articles, etc.

You may not make a lot of money writing a book, but the mileage you can get out of it is worth all the aggro.

# 7

# How to keep in touch

What's the biggest problem facing you when you are looking for new business opportunities?

- A Identifying prospects?
- B Getting appointments?
- C Conducting the interview?
- D None of the above?

I suggest the answer is D. It's building and maintaining a relationship. And it starts with handling the response to the following line: 'Well, that's very interesting. Thanks for dropping in. I don't have anything for you right now, but do keep in touch.'

Knowing how to keep in touch (KIT) and how to care for and feed your clients is one of the most important activities in your business dealings.

It's a well-known fact that many sales are not completed on the first call. It's not so well known that many sales are not completed until the *13th* call. So this section is about how to KIT – without being a nuisance.

# LEND YOUR PROSPECT SOMETHING THAT MUST BE RETURNED

When I was screening excerpts from videos I had created, with the head of in-house video at a major bank, the prospect became very interested in one tape: *Your Guide to Antique Shopping in Britain*. He was fascinated with the subject of antiques and wanted to see more. The programme is an hour long.

'Would you like to borrow it?' I said. Later, I called back to thank him for returning the tape and asked him how he enjoyed it. 'You loved it? Great! By the way...'

# CALL BEFORE OR AFTER HOURS TO BYPASS THE SECRETARY/PA

If the secretary or PA starts work at 9 am, call your prospect at 8.30. If the secretary quits at 5.30, call your prospect at 6 pm. Chances are the prospect will answer the phone.

# GET YOUR PROSPECT'S PERSONAL DIRECT NUMBER AND USE IT, BUT DON'T ABUSE IT

If you are dealing with big enough shots, they may have a direct telephone on their desk that bypasses the company switchboard. The idea on incoming calls is that only they answer it. So if it's you on the other end, you'd better have a good reason to call. A simple KIT call ain't good enough. They'll have the number changed!

# GET TO KNOW THE SECRETARY/PA VERY WELL

Good secretaries/PAs are worth their weight in gold. They are interesting people who should be cultivated. Find out when their birthdays are and send them cards. Bring in flowers to acknowledge special treatment. Make them your partner in dealing with their boss. *KIT* them!

I always make a point of getting the secretary/PA's name on initial contact. Then in my personal telephone listings and prospect databases I list the PA's name right along with the target's.

# LEAVE A COMPELLING MESSAGE TO ENSURE A CALL BACK

Unless you are a really important person, a totally fascinating conversationalist or a really good friend, it's sometimes hard to penetrate the secretary/personal assistant/switchboard barrier if you're just calling to KIT. This is especially true if your prospect is 'in a meeting' or 'on the other line'. How can you make him or her call back? Less than 20 per cent of people return calls to people like us (I made that statistic up, but it sounds right, doesn't it?).

When you are asked to leave a message, as well as your name and number leave a subject that will trigger a response. You may even leave a deadline. 'Please tell her I need her input for this article I'm writing for [important publication] on [what she does], and I'm on deadline, so I need to hear back from her before 4 o'clock.'

# DEVELOP A REASON TO CALL BACK

Every KIT communication should evolve into an ongoing dialogue that continues over the days, weeks and months. So you need to derive a reason for prospects to *want* you to call back, so that they are *expecting your call* and leave strict instructions to be *interrupted* when you call, because it's *that* important. It could be the date of an event, a telephone number, the name of a book, the name of a product, the dealer who sells it, the reaction of a friend who uses it – something that only you can supply, which they want, but that you have to get back to them on. The trick is to do this every time, so there's *always* a reason to take your call.

# NEVER ASSUME

If you are involved in a communication, never assume that it got through just because you sent it. This is especially true of faxes. Sending a fax does not mean receiving a fax. I once sent one to a client on a tight deadline at a weekend. After three hours he hadn't called back with his comments, so I phoned him. He said, 'Where the hell is it? I've been waiting!' It turned out I had the wrong number. What's even worse is that the wrong number was also a fax, and on the following Monday we got a fax from some mystery company wondering what this strange fax was all about. The same applies to e-mails.

# REMEMBER, IT'S A NUMBERS GAME

When I was in charge of sales training at Merrill Lynch in Toronto, I started a programme where we rewarded new brokers for making phone calls rather than for getting business. What we knew was that if you made 100 calls, you would get to see three people. If you saw three people, you would open two accounts. A year later, one of those would still be a good customer. The problem was that making a lot of phone calls and getting nowhere was demoralizing. The constant rejection was tough to take. But by changing the dynamic to one where the job was to make calls, not to open accounts, it became much easier for them. And sure enough, when they opened an account, it was like a bonus. It made them feel good, and this had a positive effect on the way they worked: soon they were opening four accounts for every 100 calls. So when you are in KIT mode and you just can't get through, put a notch on your phone and dial the next number.

# IF YOU JUST CAN'T GET THROUGH, LIGHTEN UP

Let's say you want to KIT this prospect, and he just won't return your calls. Ten times out of ten. You've tried everything. You've called at 8 am, you've called at 6 pm, you've faxed and e-mailed him with the purpose of your call. It isn't very difficult to get yourself into a mode of outrage at the churlish treatment you're receiving. You start thinking of calling his boss and complaining (surely he'll return your calls then? You bet – right out the window!). You start leaving sarcastic – even rude – messages. Well, here's some sound advice. Forget him. He's not worth your time. Put a notch on your phone and dial the next number. Strike him off your list. That way you win. Consign him to the losers tip. Only winners get to deal with *you*!

# ASK QUESTIONS

Don't be on *send* all the time. Sometimes you have to switch to *receive*. You must gauge the conversation and track it in the direction it's going. One time, we went on a new business pitch that included a capabilities presentation on slides. There were three of us, all big shots. We sat down in the conference room, had a cup of coffee, made the small talk and very soon the prospect started pouring his heart out. It didn't take very long to get an idea of what he wanted, and we started talking about how we could address these needs. The meeting went on for over an hour and the prospect started to get restless, so we began making moves to leave. 'But wait,' said one of my colleagues, 'we haven't shown the slides!'

The point is, we were past the slides stage and into the meat of the discussion. Don't try to get yourself back on a track you don't need to be on any more.

# GET OUT OF THE OFFICE

Meetings on neutral ground allow you to focus on the relationship. Interruptions are cut out and you can concentrate on your objectives. Go for a stroll around the park, have lunch in a restaurant or club, meet for coffee in a hotel lounge or even for a drink in a bar or pub.

# BE AN EXTREMELY GOOD JOKE TELLER

If you gauge that your prospects have a ready sense of humour, and you are an extremely good teller of jokes, try a few in an early meeting. If the prospects fall to the floor with uncontrollable delight, tell them you have more where that came from, but you are a little pressed for time right now, so you'll get back to them.

# DON'T CON YOUR WAY ON TO THE PHONE

When I was head of advertising at Merrill Lynch in New York, one day my phone rang and my secretary said, 'It's the state police!'

Dropping everything, I raced for the phone, mentally going through what transgression I could have committed (I was an alien, after all). I picked up the phone: 'This is Tim Foster.'

'Hi there, Mr Foster, this is Sergeant Kendrick of the Florida State Po-lice.' (Florida? I hadn't been to Florida for years!)

'Yes?'

'We'd sure like for you to buy some advertising in our State Police Year Book. A page is just $300...'

I know some women who cold-call top male executives. They're speaking to the PA: 'It's Miranda calling. No, just tell him Miranda. *He*'ll know.'

Of course, you could make it part of your business strategy to get past the PA in this way. What if you called your organization the National Credit Agency, or the Bank? 'It's the Bank calling...' Or the Clinic?

You may get through, but that's probably all you'll get.

# 8

# How to demonstrate commitment

The only way to build credibility for what you offer is to make every experience of dealing with you positive and unforgettable. You want to make sure your proposition works! It must be bombproof.

You must do things like delivering on, or ahead of, deadline. You must always exceed expectations. You should reinforce the positive reactions, and don't even let a negative reaction occur, but if it does, fix it, and fix it fast!

It is the accumulation of experiences that establishes a primary image of credibility for you in the mind of your target. The image you establish will help to induce further experience of your products and services. Or it won't.

You want them to say of you, 'You know, they're pretty good. They are a perfect example of the kind of thing we need in this area. There should be more like them.' What it all boils down to is commitment. Wouldn't life be great if everybody you dealt with obeyed these?

# THE 10 COMMANDMENTS OF COMMITMENT

1. Thou shalt not make promises unless thou canst keep them. Thou shalt always do what thou sayest thou wilt do.

2. Thou shalt meet or beat all thy deadlines or thou shalt be as good as dead.

3. Thou shalt act as if there is no 'Plan B', but thou shalt have a 'Plan B' nevertheless. Mayhap thou wilt fain need it.

4. Thou shalt complete thy tasks with as much enthusiasm as thou displayed when thou hast said thou wouldst perform them.

5. Thou shalt not plead false excuses, not ever. Thou shalt thus forswear artifice.

6. Thou shalt never subscribe to the philosophy that the job is not done until thou hast come up with a jolly good reason as to why the job is not done.

7. Thou shalt understand and accept verily that the result is everything and the process is nothing.

8. Thou shalt banish mystery, hence misery, from thy clients' expectations in all that thou dost.

9. Thou shalt always inform thy client when thou canst not fulfil a promise – yea, e'en before the failure occurs.

10. Thou shalt obey the teachings of Yoda: 'There is no "try". There is only "do" or "not do".'

# COMMITMENT COMMENTARY

1. *Thou shalt not make promises unless thou canst keep them. Thou shalt always do what thou sayest thou wilt do.*

If you are not going to do something, why say you will? If you say you're going to do something, you must do it! What you must deliver is reliability. Y          nts need to feel that you are WYSIWYD – what you          ou do. There can be no doubt about this.

2. *Thou shalt meet or beat all thy deadlines, else you shalt be as good as dead.*

People seem to think it is all right not to meet a deadline. Yet there's nothing worse than failed expectations of delivery. If you've bought a sofa and stayed home all day waiting for it to be delivered, only to find out at 5 pm that they're not coming, you'll know what I mean. If you're going to miss your deadline, how difficult is it to make a call to advise that your delivery will be different from that promised? Why do people leave the client hanging? Remember, you don't make any friends by screwing up like this. And people tend to share bad news with their colleagues 10 times more than they share good news. How much do you want to be shared as bad news?

3. *Thou shalt act as if there is no 'Plan B', but thou shalt have a 'Plan B' nevertheless. Mayhap thou wilt fain need it.*

This is about redundancy of systems. Aeroplanes have double and triple back-ups in their autopilots, instruments and navigation devices. You don't want to crash because of a minor gyro failure, do you? There has to be a fail-safe capability. This equally applies in all the work you do. Always have a back-up. Your scenario should go like this:

'If everything clicks, we deliver on time and on budget.'

'If this [bad thing] happens, we will do this [corrective action].'

'If this [another bad thing] happens, we will do this [different corrective action].'

Part of your task is to monitor the project to ensure compliance with the schedule and to have early warning of problems. For an exercise in this that will have you riveted to your seat, see Ron Howard's excellent movie *Apollo 13*.

4. *Thou shalt complete thy tasks with as much enthusiasm as thou displayed when thou hast said thou wouldst perform them.*

   It's very easy to display excitement about a project when you are in the briefing mode. But what you must do is carry that through to the awful moment of truth, when you have to do the work. Sustaining enthusiasm is not easy, but if you practise, it becomes easier. There is nothing wrong with enthusiasm. And there is everything wrong with a lack thereof.

5. *Thou shalt not plead false excuses, not ever. Thou shalt thus forswear artifice.*

   What is the world's favourite excuse? How about 'It's not my fault' or the standard of the building trade, 'We had a flat tyre'?

6. *Thou shalt never subscribe to the philosophy that the job is not done until thou hast come up with a jolly good reason as to why the job is not done.*

   There must be a saying to which many people subscribe as they seek an easy way out of disappointment. Somehow they have a belief that if there is a good, sound, plausible reason for non-delivery, they have done the job. The saying is 'The job is not done until you have come up with a really good reason as to why the job is not done.' This is wrong. Were you hired to deliver or to screw around?

7. *Thou shalt understand and accept verily that the result is everything and the process is nothing.*

   Reasons and excuses are process. Process is not delivery. Process is not result. Only result is result.

8. *Thou shalt banish mystery, hence misery, from thy clients' expectations in all that thou dost.*

   Do you hate to be kept waiting? Do you enjoy the uncertainty of a sudden huge tailback on the motorway? Is sitting in the airliner on the ground for half an hour, waiting for take-off, with no word as to what is happening, your thing? Then why should your client be left in the dark?

9. *Thou shalt always inform thy client when thou canst not fulfil a promise – yea, e'en before the failure occurs.*

   How difficult is it to make a quick phone call to give a progress report? Or to send an e-mail? You may even have to revise a deadline. Better to do it here than after you failed to meet it.

10. *Thou shalt obey the teachings of Yoda: 'There is no "try". There is only "do" or "not do"'.*

    My dictionary defines the word 'try' as 'to make an effort to do; attempt; endeavour'. Is this delivery of the result? I don't think so. The next time you ask someone to do something and they say, 'I'll try', check how this makes you feel. Where's the commitment? The trier is building a set-up for failure. The trier's only commitment is to make an effort to do, attempt, endeavour. It is not a commitment to succeed.

# 9

# How to build your credibility even more

## GIVE HIM SOME INTELLIGENCE

As you move through *your* world, be mindful of your *prospect*'s world. If you hear something that your prospect's competitor is doing, call him up and tell him about it. Make sure you have your facts right. 'Did you see that SoSo-FM has taken the billboard across from the railway station and they're broadcasting from it?'

## FAX HER A CLIPPING OR A NOTE

When you see a story that would be important or interesting to your prospect in today's paper or the latest issue of an important magazine, fax it to her immediately, with a personal note. You are thinking of her needs and will be remembered.

What did we do before faxes were invented? Some of your

contacts have their own fax sitting right there near their office. Use that, rather than the big one in the mail room. A fax here and there that's relevant and interesting will do a good KIT job. But don't send 17-page faxes unsolicited! You'll be hated. Just KISS (keep it simple, stupid).

## DEVELOP A PROJECT NEEDING INPUT FROM THE PROSPECT

I was invited to make a speech to the Writers' Group of the International Visual Communications Association (IVCA), of which I was a member. Most of my prospects were also members. When I needed some background information for the speech, I contacted several of my prospects to get their input, and used it in the speech. (It was about keeping in touch…) People like to be considered as experts and to offer their advice. 'I'm doing this speech to the IVCA tonight, and I'd like your advice. By the way…'

## FEED THE RESULTS OF THE PROJECT BACK TO THEM AND OTHERS

I gave the speech and saw an opportunity to turn it into an article in *The IVCA Magazine*. (The editor was at the meeting, pleading with the audience for contributions, so I offered to do one based on the evening's speech. It was readily accepted.)

When the story appeared, I sent photocopies to the prospects who had helped, with a note: 'Thank you for your contribution to this speech. By the way…' I also sent photocopies of the story to my other prospects with a note: 'I thought you might be interested in this article of mine that recently appeared in *The IVCA Magazine*. By the way…'

# SEEK AND USE TESTIMONIALS

Which is more credible to the ears of the listener? You saying how great you are? Or some independent authority saying how great you are?

Collect your fan mail. If, when you deliver, your clients give you a rave thank-you, ask if you can quote them on that. I have a section on my Web site called 'Client Comments'. It appears on many of my Web pages as a box containing a few words from a client. The comment changes every three seconds and the client is identified. Here are some real-life examples that run on my site:

- 'It's a wonderfully quick and responsive service, and it's always useful to have someone "brand savvy" at the other end of the phone.'

- 'This information has been fantastic, it is exactly what we were looking for!'

- 'A great service – no agency should be without it.'

- 'Oh my goodness! We were pleasantly shocked this morning at the rapidity of your service. Thank you so much for your help!'

- 'It's a very important tool to develop new business and understand a category worldwide.'

- 'One of the most useful sites for adpeople on the whole Web.'

- 'A treasure trove of information, easily accessible at very reasonable prices.'

- 'A fast, efficient and friendly service, thank you so much for your help.'

- 'Extraordinarily fast and very thorough.'

- 'I was very satisfied by the service that you performed for us. It was quick, precise and cost-effective, too.'

- 'An easy-to-use site – we were immediately comfortable that we had access to a professional and knowledgeable resource.'

This feature is one of the most important in my self-marketing activity. Many new clients remark that reading these comments helped them build confidence in our proposition, especially when they recognized the name and agency of the quoter.

If you have a bricks-and-mortar lobby, put up a large picture frame containing the actual letters from clients. You wouldn't hire a live-in nanny for your one-year-old baby without checking references, would you?

## DON'T BE AFRAID TO ASK FOR REFERRALS OR INTRODUCTIONS

If you do have a good relationship, don't be afraid to ask for referral business. I am amazed at how many times I have asked for a referral and got a very good one, leading to good business, which would have never happened if I hadn't posed the question. There's an implied third-party endorsement that helps, too.

## IDENTIFY A PERSON YOU KNOW THE PROSPECT WANTS TO MEET AND INVITE THEM BOTH TO LUNCH

If you are a good networking person, your conversation will get on to mutual acquaintances and contacts. It turns out that your prospect wants to meet a person you know. You be the *connector* and, if you're really broke, you can say, 'Let me introduce you to Charlie. How would you like me to bring him round for lunch at your club?'

Being a connector is a very important part of what must be your ongoing networking activity. You become known as the person who can make useful introductions. In so doing you become a valuable contact for your contacts, and they'll be asking *you* for help.

# DEVELOP A RESEARCH PROGRAMME

Create a research project. It's amazing how valuable this concept can be. In order to obtain the findings, you need to talk to your prospects. So what's the research about? It should be relevant to the industry you work in or that your prospects work in. What is it that people would like to know about that industry? What findings would drive a good *story*?

A training company might want to know how its customers allocate their training resources. An airline might want to know how many trips its best customers take a year. A car dealership might want to know what its customers think of its service. A publisher of children's books might want to know about children's reading skills.

You then contact your prospects to interview them for the research and promise to get back to them with the results later – another reason to call. The results can then be turned into an article, which you can reprint and circulate to your prospects. If it's significant enough information, you can become identified with the research and thus be an expert whom people want to quote or interview on television.

As an exercise, look through the pages of a quality daily newspaper, and see if you can identify the stories that started out as the result of someone doing some research. I bet you'll be impressed.

# INVITE YOUR PROSPECTS OVER AND MAKE A PRESENTATION

Now you've done your research, turn it into a report, with computer or photo slides or overhead transparencies. Contact your prospects and invite them to attend. Invite the press. The trade publications may well be interested in sending a journalist. You could arrange an interview so they can develop the story. Suggest interviews with one or two of your prospects, if relevant. Be the connector.

# GET INTERVIEWED ON THE RADIO OR TV

On what programmes would a chat with you be interesting? Local programmes? Magazine shows? Business programmes? You name it. Contact the news directors, producers or programme managers of the stations on your target list and suggest the idea. I did all kinds of radio interviews, some over the phone, some live, for my antiques video. In my case, we always offered their listeners one free tape, which helped get us aired. (There are public relations consultants who can get you this kind of placement.)

When I was at Merrill Lynch, we employed my good friend Ann Benson to present a series of seminars around the United States on investment know-how for women. Ann, one of the great people of the world, would always precede her seminar with pre-arranged appearances on afternoon local TV and radio chat shows. She was so credible and full of knowledge that she would often cause major phone problems downtown when they gave out the number of the local Merrill Lynch office to let people arrange to attend her talks.

# TAKE ADVANTAGE OF THE INTERVIEW TO KIT

One interview I did live was on Radio Sussex, in Brighton. Coming up that weekend was the Brighton Antiques Fair, run by Caroline Penman. She's a good customer of mine and sells a lot of my tapes. As I started driving down to Brighton, an idea hit me. I called her on my car phone and said I was going to appear on Radio Sussex in an hour. I would mention her fair, so could she 1) give me some free tickets to offer over the air, and 2) offer a discount on my tape to anyone who mentioned hearing about it on the show? Of course. Caroline dropped everything and she and I met somewhere *en route* 30 minutes later in our matching Mercedes estates, as I made my way to Brighton for the live programme. She handed over the tickets like some Berlin Wall prisoner-exchange thing, and off I went to play boy broadcaster. Talk about a KIT exercise!

## GO FOR AN AWARD

Many professions and occupations have awards programmes. Perhaps you could enter some of your work. The trouble is that this can get a little expensive. They usually want an entry fee of £100 or so. Hint: neatness counts. There's no doubt that winning an award enhances your stature. And it gives you something to put in your reception area or hang on your office wall.

## BECOME AN AWARDS JUDGE

As you become elevated within your profession, it shouldn't become too difficult to become one of those erudite people who sit in judgement of an awards event. You'll at least be written up in the awards banquet programme. It's also a good way of getting up to speed on what's being done in your industry. ('They think *this* is an award winner?')

## GIVE AN AWARD

Everyone likes to win an award. It might be simply 'best mum on the block' or 'best essay'. If it's a form of professional recognition, so much the better. Go into the lobby of any good video production company and you will find plaques, statuettes, cups, goblets and platters galore, acknowledging the fact, for example, that *The Generating Game* won the IVCA Award of Excellence in the Corporate Image Category, sponsored by *Audio Visual* magazine (produced by Michael Kann Associates for the Central Electricity Generating Board).

*PR Week*, the journal of the public relations industry, holds the annual *PR Week* Awards programme. This offers recognition in 23 categories, plus the Grand Prix. The categories are:

- outstanding individual contribution;
- consultancy of the year;
- best in-house department;
- best regional consultancy;
- best new consultancy;
- best investor relations campaign;
- best international campaign;
- best business campaign;
- best consumer campaign;
- best healthcare campaign;
- best corporate community involvement campaign;
- best non-commercial campaign;
- best promotional campaign;
- best use of research;
- best political campaign;
- best employee communications;
- best use of design;
- best use of photography;
- best use of video;
- best use of sponsorship;
- best annual report;

- best crisis management campaign;

- best staff development programme.

Many of these awards are in turn sponsored. So the outstanding individual contribution award one year was sponsored by the Mistral Group, a consortium of consultancies. A team of judges looks at submissions (each of which has to be accompanied by an entry fee). They make their choices, and then the whole event is staged at a suitable black-tie dinner held at the Grosvenor House Hotel. It's entirely self-supporting (there's no such thing as a free dinner).

Said *PR Week* editor, Stephen Farish:

Holding an awards programme of this type helps position *PR Week* as the key journal of our industry. It provides an opportunity for us all to highlight good practice and to give recognition where deserved. We aim, with these awards, to set a benchmark for quality. Our judges are very demanding, and will bypass a slickly produced submission for one that demonstrates strategic thinking, wisely spent budgets and concrete results.

Another thing the awards programme enables is the production of a fat issue of the magazine, well supported by advertising, to report on the awards event! The issue becomes a useful reference work for the future.

Almost every industry has (or could have) an awards programme. Here are a few others:

- the Best Factories Awards (*Management Today*);

- the British Housebuilder of the Year Awards (New Homes Marketing Board);

- Drinks Advertising Awards (*Off Licence News*);

- the Financial Services Advertising Awards (*Money Marketing*);

- the IPA Media Award (Institute of Practitioners in Advertising/ *Campaign*);

- the MacUser Awards (*MacUser*);

- the National Media Mind Competition (*Media Week*);

- the Recruitment Industry Awards (IPA/Institute of Personnel Management);

- the Travel Awards (*Travel Trade Gazette*).

And let us not forget the Nobel Peace Prize, endowed by Alfred Bernhard Nobel, the man who invented dynamite (get it?). Actually the Nobel Foundation awards four other prizes as well, for physics, chemistry, medicine and literature. Is there an award for your industry? Want to start one?

I did. When I launched the ADSlogans Web site, I made sure that reposed thereon was 'The Advertising Slogan Hall of Fame'. I put together a panel of name-brand advertising experts and we voted on 84 nominated slogans. Of these, 56 made it into the Hall of Fame, led by the immortal 'Beanz Meanz Heinz'. We issued a press release. We got half a page in the *Independent*, almost a whole page in the *Sun*, five minutes on *Sky News*, another five minutes on *Media Television* and numerous smaller items in the press.

# BECOME A TEACHER

If you are regarded as a bit of an expert in your field, perhaps it is appropriate for you to share some of your knowledge and ideas. In what situations could you impart this? In adult education? In courses for your clients' junior employees? In courses you develop and organize yourself? At a supplier? A little research might pay off. You'll expand your own knowledge (the best way to learn something is to teach it), serve your fellow human beings and maybe even make a bit of money, to boot!

# BE PART OF THE SOLUTION, NOT PART OF THE PROBLEM

Cable News Network's Ted Turner has a sign on his desk: *Lead, Follow, Or Get Out Of The Way!* When you are part of the solution, people want to talk to you. When you are part of the problem, they want you to go away. Of which do you want to be a part?

How do you find out? Ask yourself this question: 'Am I part of the solution or am I part of the problem?' Then act accordingly.

# SOLVE PROBLEMS INTELLIGENTLY

Don't say, 'I really have to talk to him urgently. Could you put me through?' This will get you 'I'm sorry, he's not taking any calls.' Instead, say, 'I really need to talk to him urgently. What would be the best way for me to do that?' 'He should be free in half an hour. Can I get him on the phone for you then?' The barrier becomes your partner in helping you solve the problem.

Real-life example: I went into a pub 10 minutes before afternoon closing time with my wife and two small children, starving after a morning of house hunting.

'Lunch for four, please,' I said.

'We don't serve lunches after 2.30. The kitchen is closed,' she said.

'How could I get something to eat for my family right now?' I said.

'I could make you up some sandwiches!'

'Done!'

You change the dynamic and you get what you want. The rule is simple. You say 'What do I have to do to get this done?' and doors will open for you as you have never experienced before. Promise.

# OFFER TO HELP THEM DO THEIR JOB

If they're doing a report of some kind, offer to provide input. This could enhance their interest in what you do or help them clarify the need for your product or service. Or offer to review the report to serve as a sounding board before it's finalized. Your input could be in some area of expertise in which you specialize. It could be statistics, a quote on market conditions or a chunk of one of your own documents. Ideally, you would like attribution, in which case make sure they get it right (right name, right company, right dates, etc). This is a freebie. Don't expect to charge for it, unless it feels right.

# 10

# How to grow the relationship

## THE ART OF SCHMOOZING

Which would you rather be, a supplier or a business partner to your clients? Do you want to be challenged on price ('We can get it cheaper elsewhere') or do you want to offer value added that can't be obtained anywhere else? Do you want to take orders, or to develop work based upon your advice and mutual understanding?

I think I know the answer.

So the answer to the question raised by the answer is that you must build and grow good relationships with your clientele.

It's like building and growing any living thing. It takes care and feeding, understanding and love – schmoozing. You plant the seeds at the right time. You water them and give them the right balance of light and shade. And you talk to them. Sometimes you may have to rush over and apply special treatment. But careful nurturing will produce prize-winning results. And carelessness will produce disaster.

# IDENTIFY A PERSONAL INTEREST

If you're in the person's office, look around at the pictures, plaques and knick-knacks. People like to have their stuff with them to remind them what they're working for. It might be:

- a photo of our hero in front of his aeroplane, at the tiller of his boat, sitting on her horse, walking through Montmartre, being a magician, playing a sport, on skis, in a restaurant, standing in front of the Pyramids, shaking hands with the Duke of Edinburgh...

- a plaque or certificate honouring some achievement or contribution to society, a membership, a qualification, a milestone (100,000 miles flown on American Airlines, a hole in one)...

- a model of something to do with a pet hobby...

- a trophy, even books on the shelves...

Select one that you know about and direct the conversation that way: 'Are you a pilot? So am I. Where do you fly?'

From then on, your contacts can revolve primarily around your shared interest. Work is merely incidental.

# HOW TO ADDRESS PERSONAL INTERESTS

A prospect mentioned earlier was fascinated with antiques. So I addressed his interest. Since I made the video programme on antiques, I still get invitations to antique fairs and such. I sent him a spare one, with a personal note – 'Thought you might be interested in this...'

Watch your mail; you may receive something that seems innocuous and boring to you, but it may really turn a client on who's interested in the subject. So pass it on.

Your prospect is interested in jazz. Go to lunch where they have a live band. He's a golf nut. Set up a foursome. She loves to ride. Get her tickets to the horse show. Etc, etc...

# INVITE YOUR PROSPECT TO A SPECIAL EVENT

Get the prospect theatre, concert or sporting event tickets. An invitation to a private screening. Dinner. An outing in the country. The Farnborough Air Show. Whatever turns your prospect on. When I was at Merrill Lynch in New York, nobody did this sort of thing better than *Time* magazine. I was flown down to Washington to meet their Capital Bureau correspondents (in their company jet, after being picked up at my Manhattan apartment in a stretch limo). I saw *Jaws* three days before it hit the street. They invited me to be an expert speaker on a panel. I always returned *their* calls.

# MAKE YOUR PROSPECT SPECIAL

In the rare event of your prospect coming to your office to meet you, make sure she feels welcome. Put her name on a welcome sign in Reception. But do it right. Years ago, some executives of Pepsi-Cola went to an advertising agency to receive a pitch for their huge account. The receptionist said, 'Let me take your coats, gentlemen. Mr Farnsbee will be out in a moment. Can I get you a Coke while you're waiting?' Uh, oh. Schmoozing, not.

# INVITE YOUR PROSPECT TO SPEAK AT A FUNCTION

If you're networking properly, you'll be involved in events where people make speeches. Perhaps your prospect has something to say that would be interesting to your audience. You make her a star for a little while; maybe she'll make you a star!

# INVITE YOUR PROSPECT TO WRITE AN ARTICLE

Perhaps you're involved in a publication – as an occasional contributor, a columnist, or maybe you just know the editor. Would it be helpful to your prospect's cause to pen a few words in your rag?

# ASK FOR HIS HELP WITH YOUR PET CHARITY

Maybe your prospect's company could help – the supply of product, use of facilities, lending of people or other resources, all these could become useful to your charity work. Working together on this type of project can bring you closer together.

# SEND HER A BIRTHDAY CARD

If you know her birthday, send her a birthday card. What's really amazing is how many people end up having the same birthday as you. This then becomes a special cause for celebration.

# GIVE THEM A LEAD

Your prospect may very well have to do what you do – sell a product or service – with a different audience (I sell the idea that I should write a video script for a producer, the producer sells it to his client as part of the overall production package, the client uses the video to sell her product to her customers). My prospect is the production company. Would it be a good career move for me to introduce the production company to another client? You bet it would. And I get the work that results.

# INVEST IN THE COMPANY

If it's a public company, and the prospects look good, a modest investment might be an idea. You could talk to your contact about whether she thinks it would be a good move. Does she invest in it? Ask her to have her people send you an annual report. (But don't ask for inside information!)

Back at Merrill Lynch, I was having lunch with a good consultant, Gene Casey Jr, of King-Casey, who did our corporate identity.

'Did you see our latest earnings report? Pretty fantastic, huh?' I said.

'Yeah! I'm a shareholder, you know,' he replied.

I didn't.

'I make it a policy always to invest in my clients. I only like to have clients I would invest in!'

That made *me* feel good. And *I* was the client.

# PHONE WITH AN IDEA

'I've got an interesting idea I want to discuss.' What could it be? Some way for his company to save money? Something that came up in a conversation that could affect him? A new way to tell his story?

# ASK FOR A PRESS KIT

As part of your background in learning more about the client, you might request their latest press kit. This will have all kinds of information that could help you evolve better ways for you to serve them. If it's really bad, you might even offer some polite critique.

## ASK TO BE ON THEIR MAILING LIST

If they have a house magazine, a newsletter or other regular mailing, these could be useful sources of information to help you formulate solutions to their problems that only *you* can provide.

## GET TO KNOW THEIR WEB SITE

Become very familiar with their Web site. Most corporate Web sites are terrible. Try this test. Go to any company's Web site and find their mission statement and their contact telephone number. Count the clicks you have to make to get there. Most people get fed up if they don't find what they're looking for within three clicks. And I can almost guarantee you'll find an error or two worth pointing out. One museum's Web site made a big deal on their home page that they had totally done away with admission charges, only to follow this with another page that listed their various entry fees for adults, families, students, groups, etc.

Don't be afraid to make some candid user comments if you see the opportunity – many people get too close to their Web site, or take it for granted after one quick visit to be aware of problems that leap out at a casual visitor.

## BECOME A CUSTOMER

Maybe what they do is what you want. You scratch their back; perhaps they'll scratch yours. Call your contact and ask for her advice on placing the order (don't ask for a discount – let her offer it).

# GET SPONSORED FOR CHARITY

There's always some run or other event put on by a charity that's seeking participants who will get sponsorships. But make it *relevant*! Then invite your clients and prospects to sponsor *you*.

# COMBINE ONE CLIENT'S ACTIVITY WITH ANOTHER CLIENT'S

You can take advantage of all kinds of things by combining activities between one or more other clients. Once again, you become the *connector*. You create a partnership between the clients and act as the go-between. Kodak Batteries had an exclusive at Toys 'R' Us over Christmas that did a lot to load customers up with alkaline power cells. TDK audiotapes had a deal with Pizza Hut where you get a package of reductions on pizzas when you buy a five-pack of TDK cassettes. What kinds of deals can you come up with? Your call about one of these will probably not go unwelcome.

# ATTEND THEIR INDUSTRY TRADE SHOWS AND EXHIBITIONS

A good way to get up to speed on the state of the art in the industries you serve is to go to their trade shows. You may also get to schmooze your clients at their stands. I once helped make some videos for British Olivetti about their computers. I even appeared in a couple, as well as writing them. Later I attended the Computer Show at London's Earls Court, and there I was, on the big screen at the Olivetti stand! And there was the client, appreciating the personal visit. Strike up another KIT.

## CALL TO CONGRATULATE

Keep your eye on the press, especially in your industry. If something good happens involving your client or prospect, call up and share her joy. A promotion? An award? A good review? A successful product launch? Maybe you can help extend this good news by doing what you do. Sending flowers isn't out of the question.

## CALL TO COMMISERATE

When you keep your eye on the press, look not only for the good tidings. If your prospect is dealing with bad news, call up and share his misery. Maybe you have a way to help overcome the problem. A loss of a contract? Lay-offs? A decline in earnings? A crisis?

## GET WELL SOON

Is your prospect off work and unwell? Possibly a card or flowers to the hospital would not go amiss.

## SEND HER A BOOK

When you find a book that expresses your thinking well, and reflects on your unique selling proposition, give copies of it to your prospects. *Selling the Dream* by Guy Kawasaki (Harper Business) is one I've given to people. Another is *Giant Steps* by Anthony Robbins (Simon & Schuster). Of course, since I've written 24 books, I frequently give my own!

## GIVE THEM SOMETHING YOU'VE DONE

A few years ago, I did a sell-through video called *Wheels – The Joy of*

*Cars*. It became my Christmas present for my clients and prospects. Another year, I did the same thing with my video *Your Guide to Antique Shopping in Britain*. Next year, it'll be this book, if I haven't already given it to them in some other manner.

## TREAT THEM TO SOMETHING SPECIAL THAT YOU DO

When I lived in the United States some years ago, I had my own aeroplane, a beautiful four-seater Piper Comanche. Quite often I would fly in to see a prospect, ask him to meet me at the airport and end up taking him for a little ride. 'Can I bring my kids?' You bet.

## GIVE YOUR BEST CLIENT'S OFFSPRING A SUMMER JOB

What better way to cement a trusting relationship than to put one of your client's teenagers to work one summer? This takes the art of KIT to its ultimate. Perhaps there's a project you want to finish that just can't seem to get done. Bring in the kid!

## WRITE A THANK-YOU NOTE FOR A PIECE OF BUSINESS

People remember the little courtesies. It's a fact: a good relationship with your client is more important than doing great work and having a lousy relationship.

# 11

# How to handle different relationships

## THE LADDER OF GOODWILL

Whatever you call it, what I mean is that intangible value that you own, that people respect when they think of you, your products or your services. It 's the value of your business in patronage, reputation, etc, over and beyond its tangible assets.

Yes, goodwill is an intangible, and it can become very valuable. Yet it's hard to measure it in financial terms. You can't go out and buy goodwill. You have to get it the old-fashioned way. You have to *earn* it.

Here's how I illustrate the concept of goodwill in my seminars. You have this friend, and you want to buy the friend a birthday present. You are in a Safeway supermarket and you see a display of Sony Walkmans. The price is right, and they'll even gift-wrap it for you. So you take it home in its Safeway carrier bag, and think about the gift. You'd like one just like it yourself. You take it out. It's all wrapped up. It would be a shame... so you put it back in the bag. But you still want one.

**Table 11.1**  *The Ladder of Goodwill*

| |
|:---|
| **10  In position** |
| **9  Absolute trust** |
| **8  Reinforcement** |
| **7  Share the news** |
| **6  Primary image** |
| **5  Reaction** |
| **4  First experience** |
| **3  Uncommitted** |
| **2  Just aware** |
| **1  Nowhere** |

This is the Ladder of Goodwill. It's an easy way of perceiving how your relationships stand. If you work in something other than the provision of a commodity, where price and delivery are all-important, I'm sure you'll agree that doing business is all about building and maintaining relationships. It's about developing goodwill, equity or involvement for you, your products and your services, among your clients and other contacts.

Next day you're in Harrods. There, on display, is the identical Walkman, just the way you want it. Even the price is the same. So you buy one for yourself. 'No, don't bother to wrap it. It's for me.' You take it home in its Harrods carrier bag. Now it's time to take your gift to your friend. You take the gift-wrapped Walkman out of the Safeway bag and put it in the Harrods bag. And off you go. Right?

- Harrods has more goodwill than Safeway.

- Mercedes-Benz has more goodwill than Lada.

- McDonald's has more goodwill than Wimpy's.

- Singapore Airlines has more goodwill than Aeroflot.

Where is your goodwill? It's all over the place. You no doubt have excellent personal goodwill with your family or best friends or best customers. You have less personal goodwill with a prospect you're phoning for the first time.

So let's take a trip up the Ladder of Goodwill. This ladder has just 10 rungs to take you to the top. On the following pages, we'll see what it means to be on each step of the ladder, and find out the sorts of things people are saying about you at each stage. And we'll discuss how to move up from one step to the next.

At any moment in time, you are at a different step on the Ladder of Goodwill with different audiences. On each of the following pages, you can identify people in your audiences who are on the step under discussion.

Although we have 10 rungs on the ladder, it is possible to move more than one rung at a time. However, if we do this, the rungs we are jumping over need to be covered in the activities enabling the jump. If you leave a gap in the experience, it can come back to haunt you.

# Step 1 – Starting out: you are nowhere...

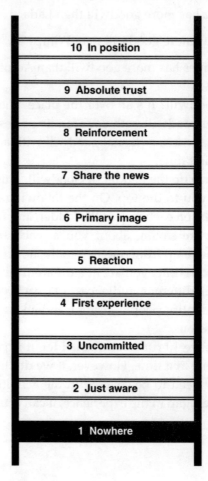

- You are at the bottom of the ladder.

- Your target does not know of you.

- You are nowhere in the target's mind.

- You must take the first step up the Ladder of Goodwill.

- You are nothing but 'Who?'

## *How you know – what they are saying*

- 'Never heard of them.'

- 'What do they do?'

- 'Who are they?'

- 'Where are they?'

## *Who's on this rung?*

List the names of prospective customers, people, companies or generic groups who fit this category.

_____    _____

_____    _____

_____    _____

_____    _____

## *What do you have to do to move them up?*

- Build awareness for your proposition.

- List people or groups who should know about you:
    - users, customers;
    - media: specialist/lay press;
    - influencers, recommenders, advisers, users' associations.

- Build a plan to carry your message, eg:
    - advertising, public relations;
    - Web site, brochures, videos, displays;
    - direct mail, cold-calling, seminars, exhibits;
    - stories/interviews in the media.

# Step 2 – You are on the way: awareness builds

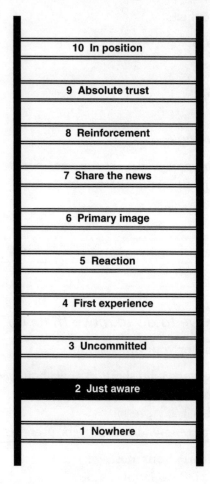

- The awareness you create is just that.
- It does not mean they understand you.
- It does not mean they trust you.

## How you know – what they are saying

- 'Yes, I've heard of them, but I don't know much about them.'
- 'Aren't they new?'

## Who's on this rung?

List the names of prospective customers, people, companies or generic groups who fit this category.

| | |
|---|---|
| _____ | _____ |
| _____ | _____ |
| _____ | _____ |
| _____ | _____ |

## What do you have to do to move them up?

- Reinforce awareness and induce a trial.
- Provide experience of your offer; demonstrate what it does.
- Network among relevant audiences.
- Develop ways for people to get to know your proposition, eg:
  - sampling, educational materials;
  - use relevant activities/locations.
- Attend trade shows, exhibits where your audiences gather.
- Be seen as the authority who delivers quality.

# Step 3 – The uncommitted

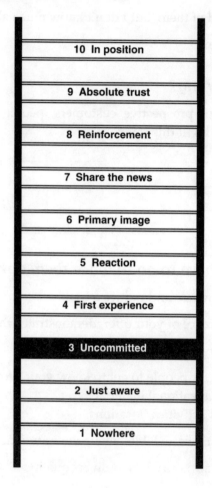

| 10 In position |
| --- |
| 9 Absolute trust |
| 8 Reinforcement |
| 7 Share the news |
| 6 Primary image |
| 5 Reaction |
| 4 First experience |
| 3 Uncommitted |
| 2 Just aware |
| 1 Nowhere |

- Your target is aware but not there.
- You are at one of the critical phases.
- Every action either builds upon or destroys your proposition.
- You must be prepared to deliver on their experience.

## How you know – what they are saying

- 'Yes, I've seen their idea. So what?'

- 'What's in it for me? '

- 'OK, you say you're so great. Prove it.'

## Who's on this rung?

List the names of prospective customers, people, companies or generic groups who fit this category.

_____    _____

_____    _____

_____    _____

_____    _____

## What do you have to do to move them up?

- Identify your key values and make them known.

- Interactive group participation of key players leads to understanding and ownership of your objectives and values.

- Support your proposition in every action.

- Tell your audiences; show you care.

# Step 4 – That all-important first experience

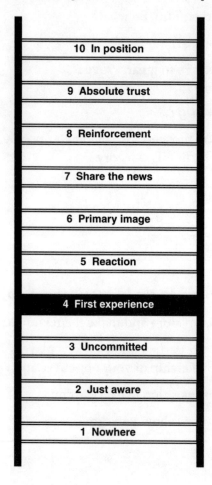

- This is the moment of truth.

- You have made great strides.

- You've moved from nowhere to an actual sampling of your proposition.

## How you know – what they are saying

- 'OK, let's give it a whirl.'

- 'I'll try some and see if it works out.'

- 'Put me down for one for the moment.'

## Who's on this rung?

List the names of prospective customers, people, companies or generic groups who fit this category.

_____     _____

_____     _____

_____     _____

_____     _____

## What do you have to do to move them up?

- Your delivery must be immaculate.

- You want to obtain a positive reaction to your proposition.

- Make the experience positive and unforgettable.

- Make sure the proposition is working!

- Exceed expectations.

- Provide 24-hour hotline/home telephone number for problems.

- Offer cast-iron guarantees.

# Step 5 – The reaction: positive or negative?

| |
|---|
| **10 In position** |
| **9 Absolute trust** |
| **8 Reinforcement** |
| **7 Share the news** |
| **6 Primary image** |
| **5 Reaction** |
| **4 First experience** |
| **3 Uncommitted** |
| **2 Just aware** |
| **1 Nowhere** |

- Seek reactions to this first experience.
- This will help you to correct any problems and build on your strengths.
- Avoid excuses.
- These reactions will go to building your primary image in your targets' minds.

## How you know – what they are saying

- 'That was excellent. I'm impressed.'
- 'Well, they didn't deliver.'

## Who's on this rung?

List the names of prospective customers, people, companies or generic groups who fit this category.

_____    _____

_____    _____

_____    _____

_____    _____

## What do you have to do to move them up?

- Ask for feedback. 'Were you happy with this?'
- Provide hotline/fax/home telephone number.
- Provide a way to get feedback/comments, eg reply-paid post-card.
- Employ a user questionnaire/survey (anonymous).
- Reinforce the positive reactions.
- Follow up with visit/phone call/thank-you note.
- Gather the responses and put them together in a report.
- Publish the report. Use in an ad.
- Don't ever let a negative reaction occur but, if it does, fix it and fix it fast!
- Fix first; worry about responsibilities later.
- Go back and make sure they're satisfied.

# Step 6 – Building the primary image

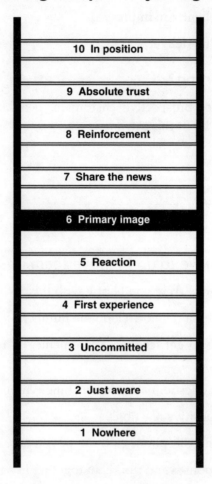

- The accumulation of experience up to this point establishes a primary image in the mind of your target.

- The image you establish will help to induce further experience of your products and services.

- Or it won't.

## How you know – what they are saying

- 'You know, they're pretty good.'

- 'They are a perfect example of the kind of thing we need in this area.'

- 'There should be more like them.'

## Who's on this rung?

List the names of prospective customers, people, companies or generic groups who fit this category.

_____    _____

_____    _____

_____    _____

_____    _____

## What do you have to do to move them up?

- Build up a file of positive experiences.

- Make this an important task; assign good people.

- Give it time, resources.

- Keep it up to date.

- Make sure all top internal people are kept informed.

- Keep the experience great.

- Make sure all components/people/staff deliver on the promise and stick to your key values.

- Fix problems fast.

- Feed back to your people. Celebrate!

## Step 7 – Sharing the news

```
10  In position

 9  Absolute trust

 8  Reinforcement

 7  Share the news

 6  Primary image

 5  Reaction

 4  First experience

 3  Uncommitted

 2  Just aware

 1  Nowhere
```

- Research shows that people tend to share bad experiences 10 times as much as good experiences.

- This means one bad experience can cancel out 10 good ones.

- Don't rely on your targets to share the news. You must do it.

## How you know – what they are saying

- 'Let me tell you about my experience with…'

- 'If you want a good result, try…'

- 'These people are hopeless. Don't waste your time.'

## Who's on this rung?

List the names of prospective customers, people, companies or generic groups who fit this category.

_____     _____

_____     _____

_____     _____

_____     _____

## What do you have to do to move them up?

- Take the positive experiences and let others know.

- Let people (customers/staff/suppliers) know what's going on:
  - newsletters/briefing sessions/personal contact/telephone calls;
  - interviews, stories in relevant media.

- Get the people who buy your proposition to act as your ambassadors.

- Make your best customers your allies.

# Step 8 – Reinforcement of things past

| |
|---|
| **10 In position** |
| **9 Absolute trust** |
| **8 Reinforcement** |
| **7 Share the news** |
| **6 Primary image** |
| **5 Reaction** |
| **4 First experience** |
| **3 Uncommitted** |
| **2 Just aware** |
| **1 Nowhere** |

- This is where you build on the foundations you have now laid.
- The more positive the past experiences, the more powerful will be the bond you build.
- You are getting close to a relationship based on absolute trust.

## *How you know – what they are saying*

- 'You seem to have anticipated my needs.'
- 'You really understand my problems.'

## *Who's on this rung?*

List the names of prospective customers, people, companies or generic groups who fit this category.

_____     _____

_____     _____

_____     _____

_____     _____

## *What do you have to do to move them up?*

- Turn a good feeling about your product/service into an excellent one.
- Don't stop.
- Make sure the second, third... nth involvement with *existing* customers maintains the standards of one with a new customer.
- Show them you still care, even though they're already sold.
- Take them to lunch, a show; give them a thank-you event.

# Step 9 – Absolute trust, or on being almost perfect

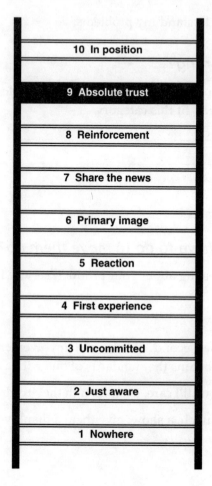

| |
| --- |
| 10 In position |
| 9 Absolute trust |
| 8 Reinforcement |
| 7 Share the news |
| 6 Primary image |
| 5 Reaction |
| 4 First experience |
| 3 Uncommitted |
| 2 Just aware |
| 1 Nowhere |

- When you have the condition of absolute trust, you can have a disaster and it seemingly won't matter.

- But it does matter, so avoid disasters.

- You are nearly at the top of the ladder, but you can still fall off, and it's a long way down!

## How you know – what they are saying

- 'These people will absolutely deliver for you. You have no worries.'

- 'I do not hesitate in recommending them.'

## Who's on this rung?

List the names of prospective customers, people, companies or generic groups who fit this category.

| | |
|---|---|
| _____ | _____ |
| _____ | _____ |
| _____ | _____ |
| _____ | _____ |

## What do you have to do to move them up?

- Maintain the relationship at all times.

- Always anticipate needs and deliver evidence of this vigilance on your part.

- Never let more than *one* month go by without a personal 'touch' with your key contacts (visit/letter/phone call).

- Think of ways to *keep* in touch.

- Scour the media for reasons to show you are thinking about them.

- Find a reason (eg competitive news) and call.

- Be the second most informed person about the contact's business (the contact is the first).

# Step 10 – Sitting on top of the world

| |
|---|
| **10 In position** |
| **9 Absolute trust** |
| **8 Reinforcement** |
| **7 Share the news** |
| **6 Primary image** |
| **5 Reaction** |
| **4 First experience** |
| **3 Uncommitted** |
| **2 Just aware** |
| **1 Nowhere** |

Congratulations. You are where the leaders are:

- Mercedes-Benz;
- Harrods;
- McDonald's;
- Federal Express;
- you.

## How you know – what they are saying

- 'Why fool around with anyone else?'
- 'Let me tell you why they are so good.'
- 'They are the best. Full stop.'

## Who's on this rung?

List the names of prospective customers, people, companies or generic groups who fit this category.

_____    _____

_____    _____

_____    _____

_____    _____

## What do you have to do to keep them there?

- Follow all the steps that got you where you are today.
- Maintain the positive relationship.
- Keep proving your fans to be right.
- Bring the laggards in your targets to the top.
- Different people are at different steps on your Ladder of Goodwill at any one time.
- Periodically analyse all contact relationships and…
- Keep moving the lower ones up, while keeping the top ones on top.

# 12

# How to work with your clients in the development stage

Notice the heading says work *with*, not work *for*. The idea is to be thought of as your client's partner or consultant, rather than someone who takes a brief and turns in a result.

By involving your clients in what you do, you build a sense of ownership. There is a lot of satisfaction to be had in working a problem through and coming up with a solution. It produces a valuable bonding that can't be obtained any other way. At the very least, it has to do with keeping your client in the loop, asking for feedback as you go along, making mid-course corrections as necessary, asking for a reality check.

And all of this contributes to building and maintaining that all-important *relationship*.

## INVOLVE YOUR CLIENT IN THE WORK

If you take a brief and go away and do all the work and come back and say, 'Here it is!', you put yourself in the position of being judged. Maybe there's something about it they don't like. Maybe they reject it. If you haven't involved them in the development, you're dead.

At least you should check in halfway through the activity and review your progress. This is as true if you are painting her living room as it is if you are developing a marketing communications programme. It's about *ownership*, of which more in a moment.

# INVOLVE THE *RIGHT* CLIENT IN THE WORK

Back in the United States, I once created a slide show for a major client. I was given the brief by Mr Big, and was assigned Mabel Minion as my ongoing interface. In my contacts with Mabel, I got approval of all the slide copy (100 slides), and of the layout and basic design, which was very elegant and classy. I sent samples of the slides to Mabel before we went ahead and received an OK. Then we made the slides, and I flew up in my trusty Piper Comanche to present the show. It was beautiful. The last slide popped through and the lights went up. Then there was an extremely long and increasingly uncomfortable silence. I looked at Mr Big with an expectant smile on my face. 'That's the worst slide show I've ever seen!' he snarled. Well, it seems he had this idea that slides should have **VERY BIG LETTERS** on them. Mabel had never shown our layouts to him. Now what? Well, we had done our part. I was happy to revise the slides (easy to do, thanks to computers), but he wouldn't let me. He redid them himself! But I still needed to get paid. And, after some uncomfortable months, I eventually did. But I never worked for that client again.

Lesson: *make sure the ultimate client is in the loop.* And keep that relationship going.

# INVOLVE YOUR CLIENT IN THE WORK – WHY

I said that this is about ownership. If you have a major project to undertake, and you do it all on your own, without client involvement, who owns it when you walk in to show the result? You do. And now you have to sell it. All the clients sit in judgement. If one doesn't like it, she'll start trying to unsell it, so that she can be right. Who is your ally in the room?

Now if you had involved the client from the word go, backing and forthing, exchanging ideas, reaching agreement as you went along, who owns it when you go in to show the result? Your client-partner. He will sell it for you. You just sit back and nod. You have an ally because you are a *team*.

# INVOLVE YOUR CLIENT IN THE WORK – HOW TO

I use my computer to good avail in involving my clients in my work. When I have to write a video script, after I've taken the brief I'll develop a treatment, get agreement to this and then do the first draft of the script. Then we go into my unique 'interactive computer-based script development mode'. It works like this. I sit down with the client (maybe two or three people) with me at the computer's keyboard, and the others looking over my shoulders at the screen.

The computer's screen is WYSIWYG (what you see is what you get). This means that text that appears on the screen resembles a finished script printed on paper. **Boldfaced** words are **bold**. *Italics* are *italic*. The layout is right. We start going through the script, scene by scene, and I read the dialogue or commentary. I ask if the words sound right. I get them to read them and make changes. Thanks to the computer, if we don't like something we can change it. It's not only effortless. The end product is a script, which looks like a script, which they *own*. And the whole process takes maybe two or three hours. I have used this technique dozens of times, and *it works*! I've also used it when writing a speech, with great success.

# TALK UP THE BENEFITS, NOT THE FEATURES

A lot of people in the early years of their careers have a problem with talking up the benefits. But remember, people don't buy products; they buy benefits. They don't buy a stereo; they buy 'beautiful sound'. They don't buy a video recorder; they buy 'freedom to watch TV on their own terms'.

# TALK UP THE ULTIMATE BENEFIT – HOW TO

I will now give you my secret for recognizing a benefit from a feature, and for getting to the *ultimate benefit*. The ultimate benefit is the most compelling reason to buy, based on that specific feature.

My secret is based on the word so. All you do is make a statement about the product or service, and then say 'so...?' There needs to be a slight questioning inflection in your voice. And you keep saying 'so...?' until you get to the ultimate benefit.

For example: 'This video recorder has its own tuner, so... you can record a programme on one channel while you are watching one on another channel, so... you can run your life on your own terms, not on the dictates of a programme schedule, so... you can get more out of your time, and do what you want when you want, so... you can be free, so...?' When you run out of responses to the word 'so...?', you should be at the ultimate benefit.

# UNDERSTAND YOUR OBJECTIVES AND LOOK AT THEM FREQUENTLY

It's easy to have a knee-jerk reaction to a stimulus, and go off in a direction that addresses an immediate problem that seems to have surfaced. But what are we trying to do here? People allow themselves to lose sight of their objectives when they get bogged down in detail.

It's not a bad idea to create a sign stating the key objective and hang it on the wall where you can see it while you work. If you find yourself wading through seemingly irrelevant activities on your way to the solution, stop for a moment and say, 'Just a minute! What's the issue here? Why am I doing this?' If you answer truthfully (to thine own self, etc) you may find that you've got off track. This little exercise can help you get back on.

# KNOW THE DIFFERENCE BETWEEN OBJECTIVES AND STRATEGY

A lot of people get the concepts of objectives and strategy mixed up. An *objective* is simply what you want to achieve. Start all statements of objective with an infinitive, and make them *measurable*: 'to have my private pilot's licence in 12 months' time' (not 'to learn to fly'). A *strategy* is how you propose to achieve the objective. Start all statements of strategy with an imperative: 'Take flying lessons.' Another way of being clear about strategy is to link it to the objective with the word 'by' as follows: 'to have my pilot's licence in 12 months' time, by taking a good course of flying lessons from a reputable school'.

# LET YOUR STRATEGY DICTATE YOUR TACTICS

Once you're clear on what it is you want to achieve, and how you intend to go about it, develop a programme and stick with it. If what you do can be made to fall under the heading of your strategic statement, you're on strategy. If what you do demands its own heading, you are probably off strategy:

- Take flying lessons:
    - Go to local airport and talk to flying school people.
    - Send off for literature from flight schools.
    - Establish budget and timetable.
- Attend Paris Air Show. (Is that on strategy?)
- Buy *Jane's All the World's Aircraft*. (Is that on strategy?)

# 'WE'RE NOT READY TO MAKE A DECISION ON THIS...'

If you want to progress your proposal, you should try to identify what the *real* objection is. Questions like 'What are the barriers to doing this?' and 'What do we have to do to get this off the ground, Wilbur?' will help. You may then find out what the real problem is. Maybe they have no money right now. Maybe they've just bought the same thing somewhere else. Maybe you haven't convinced them yet. 'Are there any barriers to us doing this?' is another good question to ask.

If you can clearly identify an objection, you can address it. And you can't if you can't. Some people have been trained not to make a decision until the last moment that they have to. This can be frustrating, because you're ready to go now. If you sense that this is the case, give them a real deadline to work to, with supporting evidence. 'I must know if you want this by Tuesday 10 am, because the firm deadline for submitting our tenders is 3 pm that day. We're ready to go if you are.'

When they say yes, get on with it! As brokers at Merrill Lynch, we were trained to confirm the order, say thank you and *hang up*!

# 13

# How to work with your clients in the ongoing stage

This section is about not taking your clients for granted. It's so easy to do. You get a new client, who starts taking more of your time. You think of your other clients – 'Oh, they'll understand.' But be wary! Predators are around, waiting to romance your old clients away from you with a little of the care and attention that you've been unintentionally withholding.

There was a song recorded by the Blues Brothers a few years ago that said it well. The key lines were:

Who's makin' love
to your old lady
while you're out makin' love?

## UPDATE THEM ON YOUR WORK

When did you last show your existing clients what you do? Maybe it's time to show some of your latest results. Too often the people who know us best are the people we spoke to yesterday. We tend to take our long-term clients for granted.

## ASK FOR FEEDBACK AND EVALUATION

Don't be afraid to ask how you are doing. If there are any problems, it's better you find them out early than to receive a nasty phone call one day far in the future. Questions like 'Are you happy with this?' and 'Is there anything you're not happy with?' are the sorts of openers that could let you know if there are any problems.

## INVOLVE THEIR COLLEAGUES

One big danger in business relationships is that people move on. They change jobs, retire, get fired, die – all kinds of things. If your relationship is based on one person, start involving others if you can. Invite your client to bring colleagues into the picture, if only to help them understand more of what you do. Otherwise you could be in for a nasty surprise if your chief contact leaves. New people might think that being new means that they are new brooms.

## TALK TO OTHERS IN THE CLIENT'S ORGANIZATION

I have an ongoing relationship with a large firm, and I do work for several people there. But there are lots of people I don't work with but for whom I could. So I recently started a programme of expanding awareness among them of what I do. I was amazed. Here were all these people, whom I knew, whom I had never worked with, who somehow had no idea of how I could help them. There are all kinds of opportunities right under your nose. Just yesterday, I made such a presentation. There were three people in the room, only one of whom I knew. After 45 minutes, I walked out of the room with a good piece of business from a man I had never met, who until that moment had never heard of me. *Don't ignore the obvious!*

## UPDATE YOUR CLIENT ON WHAT'S GOING ON

When I was a stockbroker, I found that my clients liked to get calls telling them how their shares were doing. It could be simply to tell them today's prices, or perhaps to report on an announcement about the company that had come over the news wire. Making the call shows you care.

## UPDATE YOUR CLIENT – EVEN WHEN THE NEWS IS BAD

Clients of stockbrokers may not like to get calls telling them how badly their shares are doing. But far better they should hear it from you – their trusted adviser – than on the evening stock market report as they drive home. Maybe you can evolve a containment strategy.

There's a saying in Wall Street: 'Cut your losses and let your profits ride.' Many investors have a fear of selling a stock they've lost money on: 'I don't want to take that kind of a loss – but we've got a nice profit on the other one, so let's sell that.' The unfortunate thing about this strategy is that you end up with a portfolio of losers. Which do you think the client wants?

It's about giving tough advice. It may feel uncomfortable for you, but it is in the best interests of clients, and in the long run they'll thank you for it.

# ANALYSE YOUR BUSINESS

Every so often, take a look at the business you're doing and see where it's coming from. You can do this by sales volume (in monetary terms or in units) and, if you have sophisticated enough records, by profitability. If you use a computer spreadsheet, you'll find it very easy to manipulate the figures. I use Microsoft Excel. It lets me produce charts in a few moments so I can quickly see the big picture.

# UNDERSTAND THE 80/20 RULE

Most people find that 80 per cent of their business comes from 20 per cent of their customers. Naturally, it follows that 80 per cent of their customers give them 20 per cent of their business. And yet, all too often, they find they spend most of their time dealing with the vast array of customers who give them the least amount of business. This is called overservicing. Of course, small customers can be grown into large ones, and you should concentrate on the high-potential ones. But spending a lot of time and energy on people who give very low rates of return is inefficient and may be causing unknown amounts of unhappiness with the big hitters.

# RANK YOUR CUSTOMERS BY SALES

Let's look at an example of sales analysis. You bring up your last six months' activity and, if you list the clients alphabetically, what you see is shown in Table 13.1.

The information starts to be more meaningful when you sort it in descending order by sales (see Table 13.2). (Note that the 80/20 rule shows up.)

And you can tell the computer to make a chart (see Figure 13.1).

**Table 13.1**   *Sales analysis (alphabetical)*

| Client | Sales | % |
|---|---|---|
| ABC Co | 475 | 1 |
| DESales | 1,900 | 5 |
| GHI Co | 400 | 1 |
| HIJ Co | 400 | 1 |
| JKL Co | 12,755 | 37 |
| MNO Co | 2,600 | 8 |
| PQR Co | 802 | 3 |
| STU Co | 400 | 1 |
| VWX Co | 115 | 0 |
| YZA Co | 14,808 | 43 |
| **Total** | **34,655** | **100** |

**Table 13.2**   *Sales analysis (descending order)*

| Client | Sales | % |
|---|---|---|
| YAZ Co | 14,808 | 43 |
| JLK Co | 12,755 | 37 |
| MNO Co | 2,600 | 8 |
| DEF Co | 1,900 | 5 |
| PQR Co | 802 | 3 |
| ABC Co | 475 | 1 |
| GHI Co | 400 | 1 |
| HIJ Co | 400 | 1 |
| STU Co | 400 | 1 |
| VWX Co | 115 | 0 |
| **Total** | **34,655** | **100** |

What do you get from this? Well, you can see who your most important customers are. Look at the amount of time you're spending on each, and make any adjustments you think are necessary – devoting more time to the ones giving you the most business.

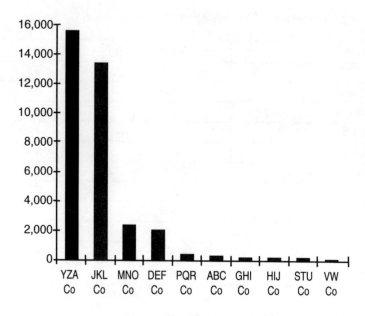

**Figure 13.1** *Sales analysis in chart form*

# LOOK AT THE TRENDS

Taking a look at the trends is very helpful. Call up your sales for the last six months, and compare them with sales for the previous six months. To keep it simple we've kept the same client list. Going alphabetically, it could look like Table 13.3. The index figure represents an increase or decrease in activity over the period, with figures lower than 100 being a decrease and higher being an increase.

Once again, this becomes more meaningful if you sort the information, let's say by index in descending order. This gives you the clients with the best increase at the top, and the worst performers at the bottom (see Table 13.4).

The result prompts a lot of questions that can point to ideas to develop more business; for example:

- What did you do to get YZA to increase sales so well?

**Table 13.3**  *Sales trends (alphabetical)*

| Client | Previous Six Months | Last Six Months | Change | Index |
|--------|--------------------:|----------------:|-------:|------:|
| ABC Co | 475 | 475 | 0 | 100 |
| DEF Co | 5,600 | 1,900 | −3,700 | 34 |
| GHI Co | 300 | 400 | 100 | 133 |
| HIJ Co | 400 | 400 | 0 | 100 |
| JKL Co | 12,000 | 12,755 | 755 | 106 |
| MNO Co | 1,800 | 2,600 | 800 | 144 |
| PQR Co | 750 | 802 | 52 | 107 |
| STU Co | 500 | 400 | −100 | 80 |
| VWX Co | 100 | 115 | 15 | 115 |
| YZA Co | 8,400 | 14,808 | 6,408 | 176 |
| **Total** | **30,325** | **34,655** | **4,330** | **114** |

**Table 13.4**  *Sales trends (descending order)*

| Client | Previous Six Months | Last Six Months | Change | Index |
|--------|--------------------:|----------------:|-------:|------:|
| YZA Co | 8,400 | 14,808 | 6,408 | 176 |
| MNO Co | 1,800 | 2,600 | 800 | 144 |
| GHI Co | 300 | 400 | 100 | 133 |
| VWX Co | 100 | 115 | 15 | 115 |
| PQR Co | 750 | 702 | 52 | 107 |
| JKL Co | 12,000 | 12,755 | 755 | 106 |
| ABC Co | 475 | 475 | 0 | 100 |
| HIJ Co | 400 | 400 | 0 | 100 |
| STU Co | 500 | 400 | −100 | 80 |
| DEF Co | 5,600 | 1,900 | −3,700 | 34 |
| **Total** | **30,325** | **34,655** | **4,330** | **114** |

- What did you do with MNO?

- And what on earth happened with DEF?

- What do we have to do to turn JKL into a growth situation?

- And so on.

# LOOK AT YOUR SELLING TIME IN RELATION TO REVENUES

If you offer a variety of services, analyse your sales time for each type or category while considering the revenues produced. Then allocate your time in the most rewarding area. Let's look at an example. We have four basic services (we'll call them As, Bs, Cs and Ds). Some are a little more complicated than others, so they take a little longer to sell. The headings on your spreadsheet might look like those in Table 13.5.

**Table 13.5** *Revenue per hour*

| Item | Units Sold | Unit Revenues | Revenues | Selling Time (Hours) | Time/Unit | Revenue/ Hour |
|------|------------|---------------|----------|---------------------|-----------|---------------|
| As | 100 | £100 | £10,000 | 50 | 0.5 | £200 |
| Bs | 500 | £200 | £100,000 | 500 | 1.0 | £200 |
| Cs | 500 | £400 | £200,000 | 250 | 0.5 | £800 |
| Ds | 100 | £500 | £50,000 | 50 | 0.5 | £1,000 |
| Total | 1,200 | £300 | £360,000 | 850 | 0.7 | £420 |

By dividing the selling time by the units, we get the selling time per unit. As, Cs and Ds all take half an hour each to sell. Bs take an hour each to sell. The average sale takes 0.7 of an hour or 42 minutes.

By dividing the revenues by the selling time in hours we arrive at the revenue per hour. As and Bs both bring in £200 per hour of selling time, while Cs bring in £800 and Ds a whopping £1,000 an hour.

Conclusions:

- How can we sell more Ds?

- What can we do to reduce the selling time spent on Bs and As?

What do you come up with?

Take a look at your own business in light of this example.

## CLARIFY YOUR SELLING CYCLE

Have you looked at your own selling cycle? What are the events that have to take place before the customer gets the goods or service and you get the money? Some transactions are immediate, eg buying an evening newspaper from a street vendor on your way home each night. Others are purchases requiring a lot of considera- tion – buying a new car or a house, for example. The newspaper takes a few seconds and is mostly a reflex action. The complex transaction might take weeks or months.

The longer the selling cycle, the more the opportunity to lose the deal. In a house purchase, you could see the following types of events taking place, with plenty of intrusions possible that could affect the transaction:

- decision or need to move and obtain new house;

- identification of area(s) to target for new house;

- establishment of price range;

- definition of requirements;

- selection of estate agent(s);

- review of possible candidates;

- selection of shortlist;

- comparison of options;

- schools/shopping/commuting;

- property attributes;

- final selection;

- price offer/negotiations;

- agreement reached;

- property inspection;

- need to obtain a mortgage – interest rate activity;

- need to obtain life insurance – medical examination;

- need for secondary financing;

- ability of buyer or seller to complete dependent on transaction (another house must be sold or bought to enable this one to move, creating a chain);

- legal or title considerations;

- need for refurbishment/repairs, etc;

- contract exchange.

Look at how many times there could be an event that affects the outcome. Look at all the different opportunities to cause a change of mind.

Now consider your own business activity. What's your business cycle like? What are the opportunities to touch the customer before, during and after the purchase? If you haven't done this before, here's a technique:

- Use 3-inch by 5-inch index cards, or a computer program that lets you organize ideas (eg a word processor).

- Put down each step in your business cycle on a separate card or line of the program.

- When you feel you have most of the steps, start shuffling them around until they are in a logical sequence.
- Identify the ways and occasions when there could be an influence on the outcome.
- Append these to the steps.
- Look at whether you are controlling those steps you can control.
- Take the appropriate action.

Here's an example. I want to write a new book. Here are the steps involved, as they came to mind, in any order:

- Decide to write new book.
- Determine competition – has it been done?
- Identify working title.
- Identify prospective publisher(s).
- Write outline of book contents.
- Define the audiences.
- Talk to friends and network about possible appeal.
- Identify potential bulk purchasers.
- Research book contents.
- Propose to publisher.
- Write first draft of book.
- Negotiate contract.
- Visualize the book, size, look, illustrations.
- Obtain visuals if necessary.
- Do index.
- Revise text according to editorial comments.
- Publish and promote!

Now shuffle the items around until they make a logical sequence:

- Decide to write new book.
- Identify working title.
- Determine competition – has it been done?
- Write outline of book contents.
- Define the audiences.
- Visualize the book, size, look, illustrations.
- Talk to friends and network about possible appeal.
- Identify potential bulk purchasers.
- Identify prospective publisher(s).
- Propose to publisher.
- Negotiate contract.
- Research book contents.
- Write first draft of book and submit it.
- Obtain visuals if necessary.
- Revise text according to editorial comments.
- Do index.
- Publish and promote!

Then put a timeline to it, for example:

| | |
|---|---|
| Week 1 | Decide to write new book. |
| | Identify working title. |
| | Determine competition. |
| Week 2 | Write outline of book contents. |
| | Define the audiences. |
| | Visualize the book. |
| | Talk to friends and network. |

|           | Identify potential bulk purchasers. |
|-----------|-------------------------------------|
|           | Identify prospective publisher(s). |
| Week 3    | Propose to publisher. |
| Week 7    | Negotiate contract. |
|           | Research book contents. |
| Week 12+  | Write first draft of book and submit it. |
|           | Obtain visuals if necessary. |
| Week 16   | Revise text. |
| Week 18   | Do index. |
| Week 30   | Publish and promote! |

The above timeline is fairly typical for a simple book such as the one you are reading. Now let's look at the ways you can touch the customer. Who is the customer? In this case, several entities meet that description:

- publisher prospects;

- the publisher who agrees to do it;

- bookshops (secondary contact – it's really the publisher's job);

- possible bulk purchasers;

- possible reviewers and influencers;

- actual individual buyers.

Timing is everything. When I lived in the United States, I wrote a book called *The Aircraft Owner's Handbook*. Because of my contacts, I was able to negotiate the sale of 13,000 copies of the book to the Aircraft Owners and Pilots Association as a membership premium ('Join AOPA and get this great book free!'). This was done after publication. Later I did a sequel – *The Aviator's Catalogue* – and went back to AOPA in advance of publication. I sold 12,000 copies before it came off the press, making a cool $24,000 on the deal. Because I was able to offer the book before printing, I was able to obtain an excellent price for them, which clinched the deal.

Ready to clarify your selling cycle? Over to you:

- What are the steps?
- In what sequence should they be listed?
- What are the timing considerations?
- With whom are the selling interfaces?
- Who can impact those interfaces?

# 14

# How to work with your clients when you have problems

Problems will not go away by themselves. They must be confronted and dealt with. If you don't control the handling of a problem, somebody else will, which may not be to your client's or your own advantage.

It's very easy to procrastinate your way along a problem, but the sleepless nights that may result are probably not worth it.

Good questions are: 'What is the issue here?' 'What is the real problem?' 'What do we have to do to solve it?' If you have bad news for clients, far better you deliver it than let them find out the hard way – such as on TV or by reading the newspaper. In your role as partner and counsellor, dealing with problems is as much your responsibility as is dealing with the good stuff.

One of my clients is in the business of training their clients to be interviewed by the press. The process is called media training. This is an intensely interactive process in which the clients are video-taped as they experience simulated interviews. Then the results are discussed and critiqued. Further iterations show the improvement that the training achieves as the day goes on. One thing that has become clear is that media training improves the relationship. And if there are problems with the relationship, media training helps deal with them and work them out. Is there a parallel in what you do?

# PHONE YOUR CLIENTS TO GIVE THEM A CRITIQUE

There are probably a few things about this outfit you call a client that could stand improvement. Does their switchboard handle telephone calls well or do they let it ring, ring, ring for ever? When they mail out a brochure, does it feel as though someone cares, or is it redolent of a crummy mail-room operation? Do they respond to their advertising leads promptly? Do they come out to service calls on time, or is it 'He'll try to get there as soon as he can, hopefully'? How is the product when it comes out of the box? Does it work, or is it junk? So, if your relationship is on the up and up, perhaps some polite comment might be appropriate. If the relationship is precarious, you may want to treat this differently, however.

# BE A GOOD LOSER

You've pitched for the business, made an outstanding proposal, you thought you had it in the bag, and at the last minute the other contender gets the job. Now what? The important thing is to maintain the relationship. Let things settle down a bit, and then continue with a low-key contact programme. Sometimes the winner will screw up, and the prospect will need a fast bail-out. Or maybe the winner's work just won't be good enough for a repeat, and you could get it next time. But you won't get much if you don't keep the relationship going.

Or perhaps you've been serving the client for some years, and it's time to renew the contract. Then they tell you they've decided to switch to one of your competitors. Having established that you can't save the business, what do you do? Maintain the relationship with your key contact people. They're not going to return too many of your calls in the early days, but if they keep getting thoughtful little communiqués and the occasional lunch, you should be able to divine if there are any problems with the new outfit. Remarriages do happen.

## WHY DID YOU LOSE?

Should you find out why you lost the business? By all means. You should know if there's a problem, or if there's some other reason. Knowing this will help you avoid similar problems in the future, or will show you that the reason was beyond your control (like 'the boss wanted to do business with the other person because they went to school together').

## IF YOU SCREW UP, OWN UP

'The best thing about telling the truth is that you don't have to remember what you said.' How do you handle the delicate situation where you really made a booboo, inconveniencing your client no end, and generally making your name mud? You own up and face up to it. No excuses. 'I screwed up. I'm terribly sorry to have inconvenienced you. How can I make amends?' This is why a good relationship is so important. Nobody suffers fools gladly, but everyone makes mistakes. If the relationship is there, you are allowed the occasional error.

## YOU HAVE A GREAT RELATIONSHIP, AND THEN YOUR COLLEAGUE HARMS IT

This can happen all too often. You've spent months developing the relationship, and it's time to bring your colleague in to meet your prospect. And the colleague completely ruins it. What happened? Whatever the reason, here you are, with a great programme that you've worked out together with your contact, ready to go, and your own colleague firmly and convincingly smashes it to pieces. Talk about split loyalties! Rule 1: Don't get into an argument with your colleague in front of the client. Rule 2: Don't let your client get into an argument with your colleague in front of you. The strategy here is damage containment. As quickly as possible, draw the meeting to a close and get your colleague out of there. Very soon thereafter, identify the problem areas and call your contact with an apology for what happened in the meeting and a promise to work things out. Then address and resolve the problem areas.

It's quite possible your colleague has killed this step of your programme's development. If you want to save the relationship, your strategy must be to start rebuilding. It's almost back to square one. And that may be equally true of your relationship with your colleague, too.

## YOU'VE WORKED OUT A GREAT PROGRAMME TOGETHER, AND THEIR INSIDE EXPERTS KILL IT

This happened to me. I was working on a script for a training film for a bank, and in my initial meetings with the clients (training manager and product manager) had proposed a way to tell the story. The film was to introduce a refinement to one of their credit cards. We'd show a teller having a conversation with a customer in which she'd be asked to explain the new service, since the customer had read about it. The teller knows nothing and promises to get some information to give the customer on his next visit. She then asks a senior branch person about it. This person has just come off a training seminar and knows all. She wants to try out her new knowledge, so she and the teller agree to go through it together. Thus we convey the information, and the customer is then well served.

This idea was enthusiastically accepted and I went off and drafted version one of the script. Now came the interactive script-development session (see page 123). The two happy clients were there and, for the first time, the experts from their in-house video production department. I thought we would simply be massaging my wonderful script, and turning it into a completely effective piece of training. How wrong I was. The experts started off, 'This won't work. We've tried it before, and we find that staff don't like to see themselves portrayed in training films. They get uncomfortable.' The two clients looked at each other, and at me. Now what?

I stayed cool. I decided it would be a waste of time trying to save the idea. 'Let's see if we can come up with a solution,' I said. There and then, I ran a mini brainstorming session, and pretty soon we evolved the idea to use a newscast format. We'd have a professional reading the news, and we'd introduce the service as if it were tonight's hot story. Within two hours, we had the bones of a script worked out, and the day was saved. Moral: don't try to defend your work against their experts. Address their needs. I did. I put them first and made it.

## YOUR CLIENT SAYS, 'CALL ME BACK IN SIX MONTHS': NOW WHAT?

You've been working on some suggestions, you've had meetings, you've made proposals. The first reaction is 'It's nice, but I want to check my budget. Let's see how the year starts off, and take it from there.' You go back some weeks later. They don't return your calls. Finally, after the third call, the PA comes back to you: 'What did you want to discuss?' You tell her. You ask for a meeting to progress the idea. Can she work it out? You agree to call the PA back. You call back. 'We really don't have any money in the budget right now for this. Can you call back in June?'

Unless you can come up with a different approach, what you have to do here is maintain a low-key contact programme. Send clippings that reinforce your selling points. Drop them a line in three months. Invite them to lunch one day. You've got to keep the relationship going.

# KEEP AN EGO FILE

This is to cheer you up when things look bleak. What you have to do is save every positive item about you and your activities in a convenient file – fan letters, write-ups, reviews, samples of work, commendations, citations, newspaper clippings, etc. The purpose of this file is to act as a reference when you're down in the dumps.

One item I am very proud of in my own file is a memo from the assistant to the president of Merrill Lynch, Peter Zimmerman, to his boss, Roger Birk, which was written when I was head of advertising at that great organization, based in New York. Here it is:

The Art Of Writing Plans

May I call your attention to the plan for a 'Merrill Lynch Video Network' submitted by Tim Foster. This plan – in its entirety – should be given to every home-office executive – from department manager up, to be used as a prototype for the writing of all future plans. Except for really major plans, senior management need only receive some form of summary. But at lower levels, the entire plan must be reviewed, if only to make certain that it has been completely thought out.

Foster's plan has been well researched, well thought out, well presented, and lets the reader know exactly what he is approving. An excellent job.

PS Not incidentally, I think the plan should be implemented.

It was.

# 15

# How to make money

## PRICING YOUR SERVICES

It is beyond the scope of this book to discuss how to price your services. Let's assume that you've worked out what you should charge, based on factors like these:

- market pricing;
- supply and demand;
- uniqueness of your offering;
- competitive pricing;
- quality;
- impact on the client's business;
- your costs;
- speed of delivery;
- degree of customization.

## Market pricing

The highest price you can charge is how much your client will pay. If the price is too high, they won't pay it. And you may not be charging enough. You need to have an awareness of market rates for your kind of work.

Once I was hired to write a brochure for a major US global bank. The draft design was to be produced by one of the world's top graphic designers. I was asked what my fee would be for writing the brochure. I quoted US $4,000. The client suggested that I should look very hard at what would be required of me, because the figure I quoted did not seem right. I got the message and requoted $7,000, which was accepted and paid. I later found out that the designer had charged $24,000 for his contribution – to produce a draft design and mock-up.

The point is that if the client typically pays a high rate for work, your sudden low rate will look odd. If it is accepted, that opens up questions about the other budgets the client is running and could upset the applecart. Get with the programme! Be aware of payment rates for similar work to yours, and charge appropriately.

## Supply and demand

If there is high demand for what you offer, you can expect to be able to charge more, and, of course, a large supply means you get less. In early 2002, Boeing and Airbus found themselves charging much lower prices than normal for new aircraft because there were so many 'resting' airliners stored in the desert waiting to be returned to service when air travel picked up.

## Uniqueness of your offering

The more unique you are, the more you can charge.

## Competitive pricing

If you've got a lot of competition, pricing becomes an issue. The one with the deepest pockets wins.

## Quality

'There is hardly anything in the world that some man cannot make a little worse and sell a little cheaper. People who consider price only are this man's lawful prey' (John Ruskin).

## Impact on the client's business

What is the value to the client of what you do? Internet guru Jakob Nielsen charges US $10,000 to look at your Web site and tell you how to make it work better. Peak-performance coach Anthony Robbins gets US $100,000 or more for a single speech. Actress Julia Roberts gets US $20 million to star in your next movie.

## Your costs

'Annual income twenty pounds, annual expenditure nineteen nineteen six, result happiness. Annual income twenty pounds, annual expenditure twenty pounds ought and six, result misery' (Mr Micawber in *David Copperfield*, by Charles Dickens).

## Speed of delivery

'When it absolutely, positively, has to be there overnight' (FedEx). (They charge more than the Post Office.)

## Degree of customization

Made-to-measure is costlier than off-the-rack.

# PAYMENT RATES

Should you charge by the hour, by the day or by the job? My preference is to charge by the job. Have a daily rate in mind, but price on the basis of the overall time it should take. Don't be afraid of quoting contingency pricing for changes or extra work that surfaces as the job continues. You don't want to get stuck with earning a modest fee for a project and having to perform all sorts of extras at no extra charge.

I did some work once for which I charged by the hour, and the billing was horrendous. The client got upset because I was charging a substantial hourly rate that made her own salary look like a joke. I rapidly switched to charging for the job.

Think about extras that could be charged separately, beyond your fee – travel expense, postage, telephone, special subscription charges, research, equipment rental, etc.

# DISCOUNTS

Most activities can support some kind of discount to the quoted fees. Discounts can be generated due to:

- business promotion incentives;
- volume of work;
- spread;
- repeat business;
- prompt payment.

## Business promotion incentives

Look at what happens in any supermarket:

- Buy one, get one free.

- Extra club-card points with purchase.

- Free doohickey with every purchase.

How does that translate to your business?

## Volume of work

You can offer a discount based on the overall gross revenues. At ADSlogans we charge a lower rate for second and succeeding searches on the same job. But we keep this to a 30-day time limit.

## Spread

A magazine publisher with four titles might charge a lower rate per page for advertisers using more than one title, with the discount increasing as the overall utilization expands to include the other titles, eg:

| Number of titles used: | 1 | 2 | 3 | 4 |
|---|---|---|---|---|
| Page rate per page | £1,000 | £950 | £900 | £850 |

## Repeat business

If the client keeps coming back for more, maybe you can reduce the rate for the succeeding work. We operate a 'continuity discount', which lowers the rate for new activity booked within 30 days of the last assignment.

## Prompt payment

Some suppliers offer a modest discount for prompt payment of their invoices. The trouble with this is that many customers take the discount anyway and still take ages to pay, betting that it's too much trouble to correct the rip-off. Not recommended. Which brings us to...

# GETTING PAID

Independent consultants are a long way down the food chain. Quite a few clients fail to realize that. They cruise around in their company BMWs, relaxed in the knowledge that their own healthy salaries will be deposited in their bank accounts assuredly on the designated day, so that when the direct debit for the mortgage payment hits with the certainty of gravity a couple of days later it is covered. Meanwhile, their laxity at processing the consultant's bills can cause much grief.

# TRAIN YOUR CLIENTS

I have found that the best clients as regards prompt payment are those individuals who have themselves worked as independents or freelancers – they know the score. Others need training in compensation conventions. Have a conversation about billing – how you bill and how you need to get paid promptly, and agree the best way to handle it.

# BILL IN CHUNKS, WITH AN UP-FRONT PAYMENT

As a freelancer or independent consultant I would usually agree a fee in advance (ideally, based on the job, not on hours worked). Then I'd bill one-third immediately, one-third on delivery of first draft or equivalent and one-third on completion.

# BILL RIGHT AWAY

Sometimes I would prepare a bill in advance of the commissioning meeting and, on getting the assignment and agreeing the three-thirds system, I'd hand over the bill for the first third on the spot and request prompt handling. I might carry two or three versions of the first-third bill, reflecting variations in fee expected (making sure to proffer the correct version!).

There is no need to be ashamed of wanting to get paid. Putting a sense of urgency to it should be couched in an expression of the reality of freelance life – always needing money.

## BE CAREFUL!

You must be careful not to overdo your need for money. I did once and lost a client because the client felt pressured. (I was dealing with the principal and he didn't like the fact that I called his book-keeper three times for payment.)

## MONITOR YOUR PAYMENTS

In my ADSlogans business I find that a lot of agencies pay in 60–90 days. The thing to do is call their accounts payable after about 20 days (get to know your handler's name) and verify that your bill is 'in the system'. Then ask when accounts expect to get it paid. Too often I've made the first call for payment at 60 days, only to discover accounts don't even know about the bill! My contact has never processed it! This means refaxing the bill and a further wait while the contact is chased to approve it.

## WHY NOT BILL THE ACCOUNTS DEPARTMENT, NOT THE CLIENT?

The accounts department ('accounts payable' or 'bought ledger') is there to run the financial side of things at your client's. Part of their job is paying the bills. So putting your invoice directly in their hands cuts corners and gives them something to do. By contrast, processing invoices is a low-priority item for many management people, who are usually surrounded by large paper piles, one of which probably contains your ageing bill. They're too busy with their meetings to deal with such banalities. Another reason to get to know the PA.

# FOLLOW UP ON UNPAID BILLS

Some clients require a statement as well as a bill. In one case I had to wait six months before I found out this gem. They often don't tell you.

After 30 days, it's a good idea to fax a copy of unpaid bills to accounts payable (they usually have their own fax number) with a note overprinted saying 'COULD WE PLEASE HAVE PAYMENT OF THIS INVOICE'.

# KNOW THE EXCUSES

How many of these have you heard? Forewarned is forearmed!

- 'You haven't been paid yet? That's terrible!'
- 'We sent that to our accounts department weeks ago.'
- 'Accounts are moving, so everything is disrupted.'
- 'We don't seem to have your invoice.'
- 'There's a question about your bill.'
- 'We can't accept photocopies or faxes. We must have an original in the mail to our Skegness address.'
- 'We only pay by statement and we don't have one for you.'
- 'You didn't sign your bill!'

- 'It's not on the system.'

- 'Our system is down.'

- 'Our next cheque run is a week Friday.'

- 'We need a director to sign it and they're all at the trade show.'

- 'According to our records we paid that three months ago.'

- 'I'm sending that out tonight, hopefully.'

- 'The cheque is in the mail.'

# BACS PAYMENTS

The Bankers Automated Clearance System is used by more and more clients, thankfully. This makes payments direct into your bank account, with the benefits of increased security and efficiency. The payment should reach your bank account and be usable earlier than a cheque mailed to you, which must then be banked. When a BACS payment hits your account, it is treated by your bank as cash, so there is no five-day clearing problem.

Put your banking details on your invoice and request a BACS payment. It's also a good idea to put the payment terms on your invoice, eg 'Payment is due upon receipt.'

# GET IT IN WRITING

Some consultants go to a lot of trouble with contracts and agreements laying out the ground rules of the gig. Consult your legal adviser. At the very least, get a purchase order or some kind of written commitment covering the engagement, fees and payment terms.

Many clients insist that their purchase order accompany any invoices. Check this out and make sure you get one if required. Some businesses also assign a job number to the project. This enables them to track their own expenditures. Always ask if there is a job number and put it on the invoice.

## IF YOU HAVE A BILLING PROBLEM, DEAL WITH IT

You really need to get these sorts of things out of the way. Find out what the problem is and negotiate a solution. If the relationship is important to you, how much are you prepared to spend to keep it? Or how much do you need to make to lose it? It might be costly to replace the client just to save your wounded pride.

## BANK YOUR CHEQUES IMMEDIATELY!

When you finally get the cheque, bank it that day! Depositing cheques is one of the best ways to measure your success as an independent consultant. Do not abuse this!

# 16

# Conclusion

## THE 16 CRITICAL SUCCESS FACTORS FOR INDEPENDENT CONSULTANTS

This book has discussed the quest for success, so let us summarize the 16 key success factors we have been talking about.

1. Plan, don't just react.

2. Never assume.

3. KISS! Keep it simple, stupid.

4. Know your USP and talk the talk.

5. Come across as a success.

6. Be clear on your positioning. Make everything you do support it.

7. Know your customers and put their interests first.

8. Promote what you do relevantly and effectively.

9. Keep in touch – don't lose track.

10. Demonstrate commitment and reliability.

11. Make your client or prospect special.

12. Handle different relationships appropriately.

13. Involve your client in the work.

14. Ask for feedback, evaluation and referrals.

15. Analyse your business.

16. Handle money issues carefully and well.

Please let me know what you think of this book. All comments and suggestions are welcome. If you *don't* like it, tell *me*. If you *do* like it, tell *your friends*! E-mail me at fostair@adslogans.co.uk.

And be a success!

# Some useful Web sites

Agents Association of Great Britain Ltd
 http://www.agents-uk.com
Association for Information
Management
 http://www.aslib.co.uk
Association for Management Education
& Development
 http://www.management.org.uk
Association for Project Management
 http://www.apm.org.uk
Association of Accounting Technicians
 http://www.aat.co.uk
Association of British Science Writers
 http://www.absw.org.uk
Association of Building Engineers
 http://www.abe.org.uk/abe
Association of Consulting Engineers
 http://www.acenet.co.uk
Association of Illustrators
 http://www.aoi.co.uk
Association of Independent Computer
Specialists
 http://www.aics.org.uk
Association of MBAs
 http://www.mba.org.uk
Association of Medical Illustrators
 http://medical-illustrators.org
Association of Photographers
 http://www.photouk.co.uk/
 assop_txt.html
Association of Professional Engineers
 http://www.ukape.org.uk

Astrological Association of Great
Britain
 http://www.astrologer.
 com/aanet
Better Business magazine
 http://www.better-business.co.uk
British Accounting Association
 http://www.shef.ac.uk/~baa
British Association of Communicators
in Business
 http://www.bacb.org
British Association of Women
Entrepreneurs
 http://www.bawe-uk.org
British Consultants & Construction
Bureau
 http://www.bccb.org.uk
British Web Design and Marketing
Association
 http://www.bwdma.com
Business Link Network Company
 http://www.businesslink.org
Chartered Institute of Journalists
 http://www.ioj.co.uk
Chartered Institute of Library and
Information Professionals
 http://www.cilip.org.uk
Chartered Institute of Management
Accountants
 http://www.cima.org.uk
Chartered Institute of Marketing
 http://www.cim.co.uk

Chartered Institute of Personnel and
Development
  http://www.cipd.co.uk
Chartered Institute of Purchasing and
Supply
  http://www.cips.org
Chartered Society of Designers
  http://designwebb.co.uk
Confederation of British Industry
  http://www.cbi.org.uk
Craft Potters Association of Great
Britain Ltd
  http://www.ceramic-
  review.co.uk/cpa/cpa.htm
Crime Writers' Association
  http://www.thecwa.co.uk
Department of Trade and Industry
  http://www.dti.gov.uk/support/
  index.htm
Direct Marketing Association
  http://www.dma.org.uk
European Association of Research
Managers and Administrators
  http://www.cineca.it
Federation of Small Businesses Ltd
  http://www.fsb.org.uk
Forum of Private Business
  http://www.fpb.co.uk
Gay Business Association
  http://www.gba.org.uk
Home Aloners UK
  http://www.homealoners.co.uk
HTML Writers Guild
  http://www.hwg.org
IEEE Professional Communication
Society
  http://www.ieeepcs.org
Incorporated Society of Musicians
  http://www.ism.org
Independent Financial Advisers
Association
  http://www.ifaa.org.uk
Independent Safety Consultants
Association
  http://www.isca.org.uk
Information Technology Professionals
Association
  http://www.msf-itpa.org.uk
Institute for Learning and Teaching
  http://www.ilt.ac.uk

Institute for the Management of
Information Systems
  http://www.imis.org.uk
Institute of Chartered Accountants in
England and Wales
  http://www.icaew.co.uk
Institute of Chartered Secretaries and
Administrators
  http://www.icsa.org.uk/icsa
Institute of Direct Marketing
  http://www.theidm.co.uk
Institute of Directors
  http://www.iod.com
Institute of Ecology and Environmental
Management
  http://www.ieem.co.uk
Institute of Electrical and Electronics
Engineers
  http://www.ieee.org
Institute of Employment Consultants
  http://www.iec.org.uk
Institute of Energy
  http://www.instenergy.org.uk
Institute of Food Science and
Technology
  http://www.ifst.org
Institute of Independent Business
  http://www.iib.org.uk
Institute of Linguists
  http://www.iol.org.uk
Institute of Management
  http://www.inst-mgt.org.uk
Institute of Management Consultancy
  http://www.imc.co.uk
Institute of Management Services
  http://www.dircon.co.uk
Institute of Marine Engineers
  http://www.imre.org.uk
Institute of Mathematics and its
Applications
  http://www.ima.org.uk
Institute of Operations Management
  http://www.iomnet.org.uk
Institute of Patentees and Inventors
  http://www.invent.org.uk
Institute of Practitioners in
Advertising
  http://www.ipa.co.uk
Institute of Professional Investigators
  http://www.ipi.org.uk

Institute of Public Relations
http://www.ipr.org.uk
Institute of Sales and Marketing
Management
http://www.ismm.co.uk
Institute of Sales Promotion
http://www.isp.org.uk
Institute of Scientific and Technical
Communicators
http://www.istc.org.uk
Institute of Training and Occupational
Learning
http://www.traininginstitute.co.uk
Institution of Analysts and
Programmers
http://www.iap.org.uk
Institution of Chemical Engineers
http://www.icheme.org
Institution of Civil Engineers
http://www.ice.org.uk
Institution of Diagnostic Engineers
http://www.diagnosticengineers.org
Institution of Electrical Engineers
http://www.iee.org
Institution of Incorporated Engineers
http://www.iie.org.uk
Institution of Mechanical Engineers
http://www.imeche.org.uk
Institution of Structural Engineers
http://www.istructe.org.uk
International Association of Business
Communicators
http://www.iabc.com
International Visual Communications
Association
http://www.ivca.com
Investors in People
http://www.iipuk.co.uk
Management Consultancies Association
http://www.mca.org.uk
Market Research Society
http://www.marketresearch.org.uk
Marketing Council
http://www.marketingcouncil.org
Medical Artists' Association
http://www.staff.ncl.ac.uk/alan.
waller/medical_artists_uk
Public Relations Consultants
Association
http://www.martex.co.uk/prca

Royal Aero Club of the UK
http://www.royalaeroclub.
org/raechome.htm
Royal Aeronautical Society
http://www.raes.org.uk
Royal Astronomical Society
http://www.ras.org.uk
Royal Institution of Chartered
Surveyors
http://www.rics.org.uk
Royal Meteorological Society
http://www.royal-met-soc.
org.uk
Royal Photographic Society
http://www.rps.org
Royal Society of Arts
http://www.rsa.org.uk
Royal Statistical Society
http://www.rss.org.uk
Royal Television Society
http://www.rts.org.uk
Society for Editors and Proofreaders
http://www.sfep.org.uk
Society for Technical Communication
http://www.stc.org
Society of Authors
http://www.writers.org.
uk/society
Society of British Theatre Designers
http://www.theatredesign.org.uk
Society of Competitive Intelligence
Professionals
http://www.scip.org
Society of Engineers
http://www.society-of-engineers.
org.uk
Society of Pension Consultants
http://www.spc.uk.com
Society of Professional Engineers
http://www.
professionalengineers-uk.com
Strategic Planning Society
http://www.sps.org.uk
TEC National Council
http://www.tec.co.uk
Work Foundation (formerly The
Industrial Society)
http://www.indsoc.co.uk
Writers' Guild of Great Britain
http://www.writersguild.org.uk/

# Index